BREAK
THE
SILENCE
BARRIER

BREAK
THE
SILENCE
BARRIER

MARGARET FOURIE

M ETZ PRESS

Published by Metz Press
1 Cameronians Avenue
Welgemoed 7530

First published 1997
Second impression 1997
Copyright© Metz Press 1997
Text copyright © Margaret Fourie 1997
Illustrations copyright © Metz Press 1997

Editor	Wilsia Metz
Copy editor	Ethné Clarke
Proofreader	Thea Coetzee
Design and typesetting	EPS & M
Cartoons	Gideon Engelbrecht
Production coordinator	Andrew de Kock
Reproduction	Cape Imaging Bureau, Woodstock
Printing and binding	National Book Printers, Goodwood, Western Cape

ISBN 1-875001-33-6

Contents

Introduction

Life is either a daring adventure or nothing.
To keep our faces toward change and behave like free spirits
in the presence of fate is strength undefeatable.
HELEN KELLER

Sylvia Horne of USA image consultants, *Colour Me Beautiful,* describes an interesting experiment conducted with five women about to present themselves for job interviews. Each woman was told that a scar had been painted into her make-up. They were not given mirrors to see what the 'scars' looked like.

After the interviews, every one of the women reported having had a dreadful interview and claimed that her interviewer had concentrated solely on the scar and had not listened to a word she said. The strange thing was that there were no scars at all – they had merely been told that there were! They had behaved as if they had scars on their faces and then perceived and interpreted the behaviour of the interviewer in terms of that belief. The facts had had nothing to do with their perceptions!

What this story illustrates is that many of us carry around with us a great deal of baggage, believing what other people have told us about ourselves – 'You're stupid,' 'You're fat,' 'You're clumsy,' 'You'll never get anywhere in life' – and we respond to situations in our lives in terms of these messages, even when they are not based on fact at all. We need to make a conscious effort to get rid of this baggage. For if we continue to be ruled by such misconceptions, we shall lose out on the freedom and wholeness we could be experiencing as adult people.

There must be many people who despair about themselves, wondering what is wrong with them. To them, others seem to be so strong and confident, while they seem always to get things wrong. Many people feel vulnerable or disappointed in themselves, or frequently misunderstood, and wonder why that should be so. It may appear to them that the people they admire must have some inside information or some secret way of dealing with situations in life that is not known to everyone.

GET TO KNOW YOURSELF

As you work through this book, you will gain the sort of insight into your behaviour patterns that will help you identify the causes of your problems, and to find new ways of behaving that will open up new possibilities. Perhaps your upbringing, or events and situations that took place in the past, have helped to build up this baggage you are carrying. And since you are unaware of much of it, you feel trapped, not by your own default so much as through ignorance.

You will also begin to identify the different choices you have for handling difficult situations. Choose what feels best for you. In each case there is a way which is likely to prove helpful in relationships and encourage you to grow into maturity and freedom. But move at the pace which you find comfortable, and always with the knowledge that you are not alone in your difficulties – there are thousands of others battling with the same issues!

Everything dealt with in this book is connected with communication, because it is in this area that we find out most about ourselves. It is in our communication that we express our humanity and reach out to or reject other people.

Communication in its widest sense forms the basis of our relationships.

STYLES OF INTERACTION

We will be looking closely at the different ways in which people interact with one another.

Some interactional styles make for good communication and clear understanding between all the parties involved, while other styles (perhaps even using the same words) lead to poor communication, misunderstandings, hard feelings and, frequently, conflict.

Words are very powerful. In a way, words are responsible for the reality we perceive – what we understand as reality is very often far more the interpretation we have put on the words than the words themselves. We could even say, then, that words create realities for us. So we would do well to use them with care. Even so, actions speak louder than words and are sometimes far more telling than words could ever be. Sometimes our words and our actions don't match, and that is when we send 'mixed messages'.

Whether we intend to or not, we are all communicating all the time. Even when we are silent or ignoring someone, we are in fact sending a message such as 'I want to be left alone' or 'I do not wish to speak to you'. These messages are not communicated in words, but in our non-verbal behaviour – body position, facial expression, distance from other people, and so on.

We can choose how we would like to communicate, but we can never choose *not* to communicate.

MEANINGS AND HIDDEN MEANINGS

When we do speak, these same non-verbal factors convey very powerful hidden messages which may either help or hinder our verbal messages in their task. Sending a message consisting of words, facial expressions, tone of voice and body posture to another person can be likened to sending a parcel, which the recipient needs to unwrap to get the whole meaning. Sometimes this message 'parcel' may be so badly made up that the other person feels the 'wrapping' is simply too confusing or too difficult to untie. And so the whole meaning, the content of the message, is lost to the unwilling, uninterested or confused recipient.

This book is intended to help you discover your various interactional styles; which of them work well and are helpful; and which tend to work to your disadvantage in different ways. We will look at techniques you can use to strengthen the useful styles; discover possible methods of getting rid of those that don't work well; and learn new ways of communicating confidently, honestly and successfully.

What is of the greatest importance is that you should constantly bear in mind that **you have a choice.** You can choose to grow fast or more slowly. You can even choose not to grow at all.

If you decide that you want to gain as much as you can from this book, then do each of the exercises as you progress through each chapter. Write the answers in the spaces provided. It may feel strange at first, writing in a book like this, but it will work to your benefit. It will help you formulate your thoughts more clearly and, if you decide to read the book again, you will be able to see how your mind was working the first time you read it. You may well find that you have moved on quite considerably. And that will give you great encouragement and satisfaction.

But remember, how you approach this book and what it can do for you will depend on you alone. The benefits you derive from it will be your own responsibility and your own choice.

CHAPTER I

Communicating in Words and Silences

There is no pleasure to me without communication;
there is not so much as a sprightly thought comes to my mind,
but I grieve that I have no-one to tell it to.
MONTAIGNE

Communication is much more than the mere exchange of words. Whenever you are with another person, even if you are not talking to each other at the time, you are communicating at some level. Apart from the words you are using (or not using), you are at the same time participating in a relationship – you are relating to each other.

COMMUNICATION CONSISTS OF MESSAGES

We call the words you say the **content message** and the sort of message that is communicated about your relationship the **relationship message.** If we were to compare the two, the relationship message would usually be the more powerful by far. Psychologists tell us that only seven to eight per cent of our communication consists of content message, and takes place through the words we say. The rest is all non-verbal (relationship message).

Let's look at this non-verbal aspect of communication first.

Non-verbal communication

A non-verbal message involves the way you sit or stand, how you make eye contact with the other person, your posture, and the expression on your face. You may even give a big sigh or a sniff. Think of a time you were with someone who did not say a single word, but you nevertheless received a very clear message. Perhaps that message said, 'I am angry with you!' or 'I'm feeling sorry for myself'. There was no need for that person to say anything

at all because of the non-verbal cues relayed to you. A silence punctuated with gestures or body positions can communicate as clearly, if not more clearly, than words.

When you interact with people, all your facial expressions, postures, movements and the sounds you make convey messages to them. At the same time, you will be picking up messages from them, whether or not they are aware of sending any.

The most important component of really good communication skills is an ability to listen; and to be a really good listener you have to practise listening with your eyes as well as your ears (see page 15).

Mixed messages

It makes sense that, since so much of a message is conveyed in a non-verbal way, it is possible to send a mixed message when we use words that mean one thing while using non-verbal cues that say the opposite.

It is particularly important, when you are in a situation of potential strain, to be aware of the relationship messages you really want to send. We have to make sure that our verbal and non-verbal messages match. This is sometimes referred to as **congruence**. When we achieve congruence our messages are clear, which ensures that the entire interaction process works to everyone's advantage.

It often happens that, while you are listening to what someone is saying, you notice something about her expression; or perhaps something about the way she is sitting or the way she is looking at you comes into sharp focus. That aspect seems to be clamouring for attention. Most often, we push it away from our consciousness and try to concentrate on the words we hear. But it may be both useful and interesting to try to catch the message your eyes are picking up and ask yourself, 'How does that make me feel? Do I feel confused because I sense something that doesn't agree with what the words are trying to say?'

 Think of a time when one of your parents, or a teacher, or your boss, called you into their room or office. Maybe they said something like, 'Oh, there you are! Come here for a moment, won't you?' in a very sweet, unthreatening voice. But you knew for certain that there was trouble ahead. We have all had moments like that. It was quite possibly not merely a guilty conscience that caused the feeling of dread. It may have been something in the non-verbal messages which spoke to us. Was there perhaps a glint in their eyes, a slight frown, or even a tightness in the voice that didn't match the sweetness? Or did they turn away from you while they spoke, with a stiffness in the body?

Briefly describe an occasion when you received a mixed message:

_____

_____

_____

_____

Sometimes this kind of awareness is less obvious – the look or attitude of the other person is not at odds with the words. It may be something far more subtle. Sometimes you may be aware only of *your own feelings* while a person is speaking, and find that these feelings are not a sensible or logical response to the words you are hearing.

Julia had this kind of experience with her secretary. Outwardly, Annette was everything anyone could wish for in a secretary. Efficient and organised, she was always there when Julia needed her. But there was something about Annette that troubled Julia; something she could not put her finger on. Annette would come into Julia's office with a smile and take her instructions willingly. She would have the work done promptly, and would have everything Julia needed for her meetings and appointments ready in advance. Julia wondered whether her feelings of discomfort concerning Annette were because she was

> *almost too good to be true – until the day she came back early from a meet-*
> *ing and overheard Annette on the phone. She was obviously talking to a friend*
> *and was saying, 'The big J will be back soon and I will have to put on my sweet*
> *face again. Some days I don't know how I manage it, stupid cow.'*

Julia had unconsciously been receiving mixed messages from Annette. On the surface all was well, and the words she spoke were entirely correct and pleasant. Inside, however, she felt very differently, and that underlying message communicated itself as well.

It is important that we learn to take note of what we refer to as our 'gut feel' – it may well be the true message, the truth behind the words we hear.

 When an interview of any sort has not gone well, when you feel as if you have been manipulated, or when someone has upset you and you are unable to put your finger on exactly what it was they said that was wrong, try this exercise. Go back over what was said, write it down as best you can, and note alongside each sentence or paragraph what you were feeling while that was being said. Compare your emotional response with the apparent content of the words (content message) and see if you can remember the visual or silent 'relationship message' you were receiving at the same time. This kind of analysis will help you to become more aware of what your eyes are already picking up, so that you will be able to pay more attention to it. It may revolutionise your ability to decode other people's messages accurately, and at the same time help you to understand your own style of communicating. It will also help you to understand why other people sometimes respond to you in the way they do.

EFFECTIVE LISTENING

Our interactions with people, especially with those who are closest to us and whom we most often take for granted, are often spoilt because we don't know how to listen, or because we don't bother to listen to people we think we know. This is particularly true when we are having a bad time, and feel that they should be listening to us. Of course they should. But the best way to get people to listen to you and really pay attention to what you are say-ing is first to do the same for them.

Principles of good listening

The **first and most important principle** of good listening is to *let the other person know you are listening.* This you can do by sending non-verbal messages that say, 'I am paying attention'. We might call this *listening with your ears, your eyes and your body*. Make sure that you are facing people when they talk to you, and stop doing whatever it was that you were busy with when they started speaking. Look at them and, if it is comfortable, make eye contact.

It may be worth noting here that in some cultures it is sometimes impolite to look another person squarely in the eye, while in others it is considered weak or even sulky not to. So whether you do it or not will depend very much on who you are listening to. Either way, make sure they can see that you are giving them your full attention.

The **second principle** is to *check that you have heard correctly* (this is called *reflecting*). We might call this *listening with your mind*. The best kind of reflecting picks up not only the content (what is being said), but also the feelings communicated with the content (the non-verbal part of the message). That sort of reflecting really helps relationship messages to flow positively.

When someone keeps on telling you the same thing over and over again, it is likely that you have not heard the deeper message that lies behind the content. That is the time to listen especially attentively, and to begin to repeat to the person what you think you are hearing, so that he or she can confirm or correct the message. That kind of listening will reduce the level of the other person's frustration and lead to really useful communication.

The **third principle** is to *listen with warmth and respect* for the other person. People will not persevere in trying to speak to you if they believe you do not respect them. Even if you do not agree with them, and even if they are irritating you, acknowledge their right to exist, to have and express opinions, by listening with acceptance. This also involves not interrupting, or finishing their sentences for them in an attempt to get them to the end of what they are saying. Listening with respect allows others to say what they want to until all has been said, and to wait for that moment before speaking yourself.

The **fourth principle** is to *be sincere*. Sincerity is associated with personal integrity, which makes others feel they can believe and trust you. Being sufficiently open about yourself reassures people so that they are comfortable with being open about themselves.

Contexts and confusion

We also need to understand the *cultural context* within which others are operating. Their cultural context may be quite different from yours and this could lead to much sad misinterpretation. Think of what we might call *culturally defined non-verbal signs* – the social rules we have relating to eye contact, or who may speak to whom, or when it is appropriate to stand or sit.

In many African cultures it is impolite for a person lower in status to make eye-contact with anyone of a higher status. In many western cultures it is quite the opposite. This could lead to misunderstanding someone's manners or attitude. Similarly, if a stranger walked into a westerner's office and sat down without being invited to, it would be impolite; while if a stranger walked into an African's office and remained standing it would be impolite. A polite African only speaks in reply to someone of higher status; a westerner initiates speech politely. In most western cultures it would be considered bad manners to waste the other person's time with small talk, whilst in many African cultures it is considered dehumanising not to spend a little time first talking about the weather and the family, for instance, before getting down to the business in hand. The eastern people, notably the Japanese, have even more rigid codes of conduct and there is much for most of us to learn if we are not to give offence.

It is vital that we try to keep our minds open to the context in which others are living so that we can make the effort to hear what they are saying and find some clarity *through the blurring* of differences.

This can best be explained by using an analogy. Have you ever admired a beautiful view of, say, a rural scene and taken a photograph of it, only to find when the picture is printed that there are great electricity pylons marching through the centre, quite spoiling the view? The eye naturally focuses on the main view and sifts out of our consciousness the familiar, everyday details that interrupt that view, although the camera does not. In the same way, once we are used to cultural differences and have accepted that they are usually around, it is possible to see past them, and to get the picture of the underlying message being communicated. In other words, we can let our differences blur out of focus and work towards hearing the real message of the person behind the cultural context.

Watchpoint

Something you should specifically *listen without* is your autobiography. It is the easiest thing in the world to chime in on someone's conversation and say, 'Yes, that happened to me,' or 'I know what you mean' and then to launch into the details of your own story.

I am sure you have met people who keep telling you about themselves when you are trying to tell them something about yourself (and usually they have found a better bargain or had a worse illness!).

COMMUNICATING IN WORDS AND SILENCES

Charles was approaching retirement age, and he had been with the same company for more than thirty years. Most staff members avoided him at social events, and had as little as possible to do with him in the office. He found this a pity, since he felt he had so much to share with them, and so much guidance to give. He had a wealth of anecdotes from his many years of service, too. If an unsuspecting person mentioned a client in his hearing, for instance, he would interrupt with a story of his dealings with that client, or someone similar. If someone complained of feeling tired, he would tell how he had worked much longer hours when he had started, and had never taken time off.

In a similar way, Marianne lost a lot of friends because of her amazing medical history. Whenever any of her friends had an illness, Marianne had had the same illness, only worse. 'My doctor said he had never seen anything like it,' she would declare with satisfaction. If someone was about to undergo an operation, they found she had already had it, but had suffered complications, baffling even the hospital staff who had never seen anything like it before. She competed with equal enthusiasm in other areas as well. When a friend mentioned that her husband was working late, Marianne's husband turned out to be having a much harder time at work and was working late every night. People eventually stopped talking to her.

> **Definition of a bore: Someone who wants to talk about himself when you want to talk about yourself.**

Another way in which you may allow your autobiography to get in the way of effective listening is by cutting short the other person's questioning or explanation with your own version of the solution.

By doing this, you are applying your own experience and what you have found in your own situation to be the solution, to the other person's situation or problem. It seldom fits.

Two unfortunate things may happen here. One is that you will interrupt before you have heard what the other person is really asking or saying, and miss the mark entirely. The second is that the other person will politely listen to you and never bother to ask again. You will have lost the opportunity to learn, to teach, or to share. If it is your child, or a close friend, you may have lost a good deal more.

When you listen, focus on the other person's story and try to understand what it is that that person is actually telling you. Ignore your own similar experiences until you have truly heard what the other person is saying. You might want to share your experience then, and you may well find, if you have really listened to the other person, that in turn she will really listen to you.

So when you listen, remember the four positives and the one negative, as shown below.

ALWAYS LISTEN WITH
✔ your eyes
✔ your mind
✔ respect
✔ an awareness of cultural context

BUT WITHOUT
✖ your autobiography

Use every opportunity you get to practise the skill of effective listening. Not only is this useful, it is also one of the nicest things you can do. You will discover that other people are probably far more interesting than you suspected!

CHOICES

Many of us live as if we have no right to choose at all. We constantly ask others to choose for us. It may be in the little, unimportant things, such as whether we want tea or coffee, or which film to see; or it may be in the really important things, such as what direction our lives should take, and what is right or wrong for us. We also blame others for what happens to us, as if they had the right to make our decisions and we did not have the right to refuse.

We will be looking at this aspect of choice extensively in this book, and I hope that gradually you will come to realise more and more how gloriously free you can be, and be able to put this freedom into practice in your life.

Holding your own

You can start with a choice right away. You can choose, while you read this book, whether you want to grow fast or more slowly. You can even choose not to grow at all. That will govern how you read this book and what you do with what you learn. But it will be your own choice and you must take responsibility for your own participation and benefit.

COMMUNICATION MAKES US HUMAN

Why do we discuss communication? What is so important about it? The answer is that it is one of our most significant activities, mainly because we *find ourselves* most truly in our interaction with others. Many thinkers over the years have come to the conclusion that we are most truly human when we are in a relationship of some sort or another. That is, when we are communicating in some way with others. A relationship may be bad or good, useful or damaging, but we will discover who we are and what we think and how we experience life in the way in which we respond to other people.

> **We can choose how we would like to communicate,
> but we cannot choose *not* to communicate.**

DIFFERENT PEOPLE, DIFFERENT BEHAVIOUR

How can we begin to understand the different ways in which we communicate with one another, bearing in mind that we may be very different people in one situation from the people we are in another?

Reflect for a moment on who you are in relation to your parents, and who you are in relation to your best friend. Or how you behave when the boss is around compared with the way you behave on holiday. It is easy to be strong with some people and impossible to be anything other than weak and submissive with others.

WRITE DOWN BRIEFLY HOW YOU RELATE TO TWO PEOPLE WHO ARE CLOSE TO YOU, BUT IN DIFFERENT RELATIONSHIPS:

_____

_____

_____

_____

_____

Because this is true of all of us, that we are often different people or behave differently in different situations, we will not discuss personality types in this book, but rather examine the different types of behaviour that go into any one interaction. We will not classify people; instead we will classify different behaviours and group them for convenience.

Building a model

A good way to go about this classification is to devise a model on which we could plot where each type of behaviour would fit, according to its attributes and the feelings that govern it. A basic diagram could be constructed by drawing two lines, one horizontal and the other vertical. On the horizontal line we will plot the way we *feel* about other people, ranging from definitely hostile on the extreme left, to warm and empathic on the right. These feelings are going to have a significant influence on the way we interact with others. On the vertical line we will plot the *degree of ownership* we have of our actions. This may surprise you, but if you think for a moment of the things we are inclined to say, such as, 'It wasn't my fault – I didn't mean to do it!' or 'He made me do it,' you will get some idea of what I mean. In a way the horizontal line shows how we behave towards one another (our interactions); the vertical line shows how we organise our behaviours (our reactions).

The horizontal line would represent the whole range of feelings, from downright *hostile* and self-interested on the extreme left to very warm and *empathic* on the extreme right. Of course, there are any number of degrees of either between the two extremes. For the purposes of this model, we could define hostility as essentially refusing to take into consideration others' concerns – denying them the right to be themselves as they see fit and to make their own choices in freedom. Empathy, on the other hand, could be defined as essentially attempting to understand the way things look from others' point of view – allowing them to operate in freedom and take full responsibility for their actions and decisions.

If, for instance, a man hits me on my head and takes my handbag as I walk down the road, I would regard that as an extremely hostile action. This man has no concern for me or for what I want or how I feel. The handbag may be my favourite, and I certainly don't want a headache!

The vertical line, showing our reactions and representing the degree of ownership we have of our actions, would run from being active at the top to being passive at the bottom. At the extreme point of being active, one would be controlling, certainly very firm and dominant.

At the bottom end, extreme passivity would express itself in handing over control entirely – merely responding to whatever others say and becoming a complete victim of circumstances and people. None of the extremes are attractive, nor do they work particularly well.

I prefer to think of the labels of this vertical line as being *proactive* and *reactive*, since proactivity implies a very strong sense of taking responsibility for one's actions, and reactivity of doing the opposite. Being proactive involves taking the risk of making a decision, and then being prepared to deal with the consequences. Being reactive avoids risk-taking and making decisions, and tends to lay both the responsibility and the blame at the feet of others.

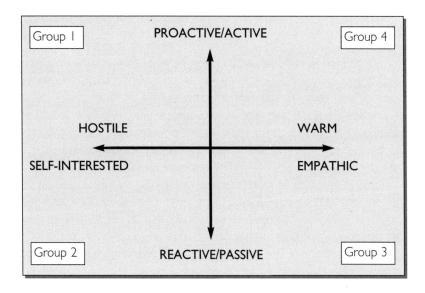

When you look at the model, the horizontal line is the line showing how we behave towards one another, while the vertical line shows how we behave towards ourselves. We can now take any way of interacting and, according to the feelings that underlie it and the degree of ownership, plot it on this model. It would fit into one or other of the quadrants.

Let's look again at the mugger and my handbag. We have already established that mugging is a hostile action, so we could plot the mugger's feeling (hostility) to the left of the centre point on the horizontal line. How far to the left would you put it? I would think fairly far over, perhaps three-quarters of the way. Now we ask, 'Is this person being proactive or reactive? Is this his idea or mine? Is he merely responding to something I have done to him or doing what I told him to?' I think he is in control here, and would place his behaviour above the midpoint on the vertical line. So the mugger's behaviour falls into the top left-hand quadrant of the diagram, fairly far over and fairly high up. In the same way we can work out where we would classify any behaviour that forms part of our interactions with others.

Being a victim

All behaviours that fall into the two quadrants lying below the horizontal line belong with being a victim. There are many ways in which we become victims in life, but the essence of being a victim is that you have decisions made for you; you don't get a vote in what happens, and you refuse to (or cannot) take responsibility for your experiences of life.

If you are the victim of a mugging, you are helpless in the face of another's decision to rob you, and you become part of the action through no wish of your own. Unless you find a way of becoming the dominant person, asserting your own will, you will remain the victim.

Similarly, we could take as an example people who have been victims of apartheid: they had no choice in the matter and were not allowed to decide for themselves. Abused children, battered wives and husbands, rape victims, and war refugees are all victims of other people's wills.

If you fit into one or more of these categories, it is very important to remember that it is **not your fault** that you do. There is no blame attached to you and nothing whatsoever to be ashamed of. The real truth about you is that you are a valued, valuable and lovable person, even if you haven't been treated that way. The good news for you is that *you can take control of your own life* and stop your bad experiences. You will find the first steps to doing that in this book. Read on and practise getting to know and love your own strengths and freedom. They are there for you to find.

A victim mentality

But there are other kinds of victims. These are the people who have a victim mentality. They imagine that people are victimising them, even when they haven't had anything done to them at all. Or perhaps they have at some stage been a genuine victim and they have never got over it. They decide for themselves that they are victims, very often of circumstances that have no real connection with them personally. The clue expressions to this way of thinking are:

- 'It's not fair …'
- 'It's not my fault …'
- 'I've never had the breaks. I'm only a woman/It's because I'm black/Short people don't get far …'
- 'Everyone always wants to rip you off …'
- 'Someone should do something about …'
- 'It's no use trying – it won't help …'

and so on. All of these examples indicate a feeling of helplessness and an *unwillingness* to take responsibility.

> *Ray was convinced that his childhood was unhappier than that of anyone else he knew. So he believed he was entitled to be morose and negative. He was not prepared to spend any money on anyone, because they had had the advantage of carefree years of growing up. Consequently, he sponged on others, smiled little, constantly criticised others and generally felt very sorry for himself. Not surprisingly, he had few friends. Of course, in his mind this served to confirm that he had been singled out for rough treatment, which perpetuated his self-pity.*
>
> *When he joined a communications course he began to discover that the people he had always envied and resented because they had had such an easy time, had in fact often been far worse off than he. He began to reassess his own perceptions of his situation, and found that he was becoming free to enjoy life after all. Gradually, he began to feel free to try out responding differently to both other people and the situations of his life, and found that, with his new cheerful, positive attitude, people began visiting him and inviting him round.*
>
> *Before, Ray had been stuck in the victim mould, and this had meant that his perceptions of himself and others were not based on fact. He had lived as if he had no choices.*

Feeling sorry for yourself tends to lock you into suspecting everyone (and life!) of being against you. In Ray's case, being unable to see the facts of his situation clearly also led to his conviction that he was a victim of circumstance – a perfect example of a vicious circle. Only when it became possible for him to distinguish perception from fact was he able to break the circle and become a positive, happy person.

Let's look more closely at how many of us confuse our perceptions (that is, our interpretation of events) with the hard facts.

Facts versus perceptions

How sneaky our perceptions are! For most of us, it is ultimately not the fact of the matter that really counts, but how we view it. How we interpret our lives has a determining effect on us, and our perceptions create our realities. We say, 'That person makes me sick!' But it isn't that person at all – it is our interpretation of what he or she does that causes such strong feelings in us. Our idea of what these feelings mean may be very far from the truth and entirely divorced from the facts!

> *All of us, sooner or later, run into someone like Alma. Alma always knows for a fact what people intend when they do or say things, and their intention is almost always unkind. She is inclined to make statements such as, 'She knows I hate pork, so what does she cook when she invites us over? Pork, of course!' Alma is interpreting as malice what may simply be thoughtlessness or a poor memory. She implies that her friend has deliberately considered what to do to make things difficult for her, and has found a good solution! Victims find that they need to blame others for everything that happens.*

Sometimes people latch on to individual words and form a perception of the meaning of an entire conversation without examining the facts first. We had an example of that in our recent history when there was a great outcry about South Africa becoming a 'secular state'. The perception that some people had was that the country would become Godless and that the church would be marginalised. The word 'secular' as opposed to 'sacred' caught their attention and they immediately launched demonstrations against the concept. Had they stopped to reflect for a moment, they would have realised that South Africa has been a secular state since its birth in 1910! Prejudice, a lack of information, and a refusal to consider the actual facts behind the perception can all lead to irrational behaviour.

Filtered logic

We each have a filter through which we view life, and which governs our perceptions and interpretations. This filter is made up of a great many experiences we have had and messages we have received in our lives.

Edward de Bono refers to 'logic bubbles'. He states that, throughout our lives, we gather around ourselves layers of meaning made up of our various pleasant and unpleasant experiences and the interpretations we and others give to them. These 'bubbles' surround us like the skins of an onion, and we perceive the world through these layers, with the result that everything we see or experience is filtered through them. If you have ever looked at something through a bubble, you will know that the curve and the colour of the bubble itself alters the object you look at. In the same way, events have value for us in terms of our own personal logic bubble.

De Bono calls them 'logic' bubbles because we base our decisions on the logic derived from what we perceive. In other words, I decide what to do next based on the experiences of my past, along with what I perceive as my needs right now. You may have had the experience of making a decision that seemed perfectly sensible to you at the time, only to have someone say to you afterwards, 'How could you have been so stupid?' It was your logic bubble operating, and from your position, you had perfect logic on your side.

Being in love is the best example of this view. When you fall in love with someone, very often there is something in your past experience that makes you feel attracted to this person, and you experience an urgent need to spend as much time as possible in the company of the beloved. You may go to extraordinary lengths to achieve this, and people around you may think you are a bit crazy, but from inside your logic bubble, it makes perfect sense!

The view from inside one logic bubble is quite different from the view from inside the next. That is why the same event will mean such radically different things to different people who experience it. You might have met someone for the first time who took an instant dislike to you. Why was that? Certainly not because of anything you are, or anything you have done – there has been no opportunity for that. The chances are, De Bono says, that you happen somehow to have some connection with an unpleasant experience as seen through the other person's logic bubble.

Now that's comforting, isn't it? It has nothing to do with whether you are a nice person or not, but with the other person's perceptions!

Unfortunately, the same is true of 'love at first sight'. The instant devotion you feel for the other is far more likely to belong to an entirely different relationship, although it may be that, given a little time, you might get to know the person and, quite coincidentally, find that he or she is indeed what you had hoped. But it is certainly not wise to build anything significant on an instant response to anyone.

All this goes to show how *unreliable* our perceptions may be. There are times when we may well be right in our evaluation of matters and people, and some people certainly seem to be far more accurate in this than others. But there will also be times when we will be woefully wrong and will feel absolutely certain that something is one way when in fact it is quite the opposite. Just how powerful our filters are can be seen in the vastly different responses people have to a movie they have seen or a book they have read. Some may praise it, while others may condemn it, and still others may have no strong feelings either way. All may be intelligent, educated people, but they all have their own logic bubble, operating as a personal filter through which everything is perceived and interpreted.

DESCRIBE IN A FEW SENTENCES A PERSONAL EXPERIENCE OF A BAD IMPRESSION SOMEONE MADE ON YOU, AND WHAT MADE YOU CHANGE YOUR MIND AFTER GETTING TO KNOW THE PERSON BETTER:

_____

_____

_____

_____

_____

CHAPTER 2

Understanding our Behaviour

Of course, understanding of our fellow beings is important.
But this understanding becomes fruitful only when it is sustained
by sympathetic feeling in joy and sorrow.
ALBERT EINSTEIN

There are many theories on the ways we interact with one another. Most of them use some sort of model with four or more quadrants or boxes into which we fit people according to their interactional styles. These models can help us gain insight into much of what we do. There is a problem, however. You may well find that the way you respond to others largely depends on *who they are*, *how they behave* and the kind of response *that* evokes in you.

Have you ever noticed how you can be perfectly assertive with one person, and completely submissive in the company of another? Some people seem to bring out instant aggression in you, while others make you feel as if it would be a complete waste of time saying anything at all, so you just bite your tongue and think poisonous thoughts! And then there are others with whom you feel at ease and who allow you be be your 'real self'. This does not mean that you are unreliable or inconsistent. Everybody has this experience. It is, I think, a shortcoming in the system of classifying people into groups.

CONSTRUCTING OUR FOUR-GROUP DIAGRAM

When analysing the way we interact with one another it is better to look at the *behaviour* rather than the *person*. Since all of us respond differently to different people, our behaviour often depends on the company we are in. You may be strong, firm, competent, even arrogant with one person, and a submissive wreck with someone else. Some people seem to 'bring out the worst' in us while others seem to make us feel really good about ourselves. How does this work? How can we understand ourselves when our behaviours are constantly changing?

How to use the diagram

The model we use in this book may help you to understand yourself. Remember at all times that *people* don't go into the squares – types of behaviours and interactions do. Keep in mind also that there is a great range of behaviours in each quadrant. The lines do not have ends – you could find yourself behaving near the middle or quite far out along any of the lines at any one time. That would affect how strongly the interaction is recognisable as being in that quadrant.

We will use the same diagram as the one used in the previous chapter (see page 21) to illustrate one way of understanding our interactions and actions. The lines are not fixed and, in each case, both vertically and horizontally, should be seen as a continuum. So the line can be drawn with an arrow at each end, showing that it does not end at a fixed point.

We may measure our *attitudes* in interactions with other people along the horizontal line. These attitudes may range from extreme self-interest and the desire to control on the far left-hand end, and become progressively more moderate as you move towards the right, until they become attitudes of extreme concern for the other person with absolutely no concern for the self. Obviously there are many positions between these two extremes. The vertical line showing the degree of *ownership* we have over our actions and reactions functions in the same way.

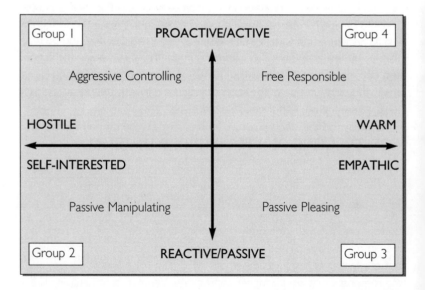

The intersecting lines provide us with four squares into which we could put our various styles of behaviour. We will call them Group 1, Group 2, Group 3 and Group 4. Very often I will use the abbreviation G1, G2, G3 and G4 instead of writing it out in full. Whenever you see that G, read it as 'Group' and remember that it does not refer to a person but to a *kind of action or behaviour*.

Remember also that there are a great many places where any action or behaviour could be placed in any of the squares – close to the centre where the effect of the position would be less extreme, or right out in the corners where the effect would be very strong.

 Of course, it is our aim to be free to choose to act and react in the fourth group of behaviours. Doesn't 'free responsible' sound like a good idea?

Behaviours are placed above the horizontal line if you make the decisions yourself, if you take responsibility, and if you remain in charge.

Behaviours are placed below the horizontal line when you experience events as 'someone else's fault'. Then you are no longer in charge and become the one to whom things are done – in other words, you experience life as a victim, as we saw in the previous chapter (see page 22).

Remember when we were at school and we learnt about active and passive voice in grammar? We were given sentences like 'The man kicks the dog' (active voice) and 'The dog is kicked by the man' (passive voice). Whatever we may think of the man and his behaviour towards the dog, the point is that in the first one the subject (man) is in control and is doing the action, and in the second the subject (dog) is at the receiving end of the action. In a way this sums up one of the main differences between the behaviour patterns above the line and those below the line.

We may use the labels *proactive* and *reactive* for the same reasons.

Proactive behaviour contains a sense of taking responsibility, while reactive behaviour requires someone else to take responsibility. So all the behaviours that fall below the line could be thought of as being those of the victim, whether by choice or through circumstances. This is because we are not in control of the situation (or ourselves, often) when we are having our buttons pressed and are merely responding to the decisions of others. We may in reality have ceased to be victimised by structures or circumstances, but our feeling of being victimised has become a habit and so we perpetuate responses that are no longer appropriate. We persist in behaving like a

victim when we could be free to make our own decisions and take responsibility for our own lives and happiness.

> One's philosophy is not best expressed in words,
> it is expressed in the choices one makes ...
> and the choices are ultimately our responsibility.
> ELEANOR ROOSEVELT

CONTROL IS HOSTILITY

An attitude is considered controlling, and therefore hostile or self-interested,
when you do not allow other people the freedom to choose for themselves
and you try to **impose your will on them**. They may experience your attitude as pure hostility on your part, even if you have acted out of a sense of
caring, nurturing interest. Either way, if you deny the right of other people to
act in freedom, they will respond as if you had hostile intentions.

Let's look for a moment at what we understand by the word 'hostile'. For
most of us, hostility denotes unfriendliness or anger: there may even be overtones of violence, and certainly violent acts can be described as hostile. But
there may be more to it than that, and for the purposes of this model we
are going to include in the definition of *hostile* all behaviours that do not allow
other people the freedom to decide for themselves.

Hostility in kindness

Have you ever wondered why you often feel so irritated when people are fussing over you? It is probably because they are telling you what to do. They are
using their own interpretation of your situation and are imposing their will on
yours. You are not being given the right to act in freedom, to be an adult, or
to choose your own response and course of action. You respond with irritation because you sense something of the hostility underlying the fussing, in that
your own sense of what you need or want is not being considered.

We don't normally perceive attitudes or behaviour as being hostile when
we know they are kindly meant. Unconsciously, though, that sense of hostility may be clearly felt if the kindness offered does not take into account how
we feel, or when people think they know what is best for us.

Can you see that, although this type of behaviour doesn't fit the usual concept of hostility, the mere fact that you are not being consulted, that your wishes and your perception of your needs are being ignored, makes you respond
in the same way you would when someone is more obviously hostile?

Most of us have probably had the 'jersey' experience. Perhaps, when you were young, you had been running around and were feeling quite hot. Your mother, seeing you without your jersey on, told you to put it on immediately. When you objected, telling her that you were hot, she replied, 'Just do it. Don't argue!' How did you feel? Probably angry, or upset because she was treating you like someone with no ability to judge for yourself. Of course she meant it kindly, and may even have been right in her judgement. But you responded to the fact that she was overriding your judgement and not considering your sense of what you needed.

> **It has been said that a jersey is a garment a child wears when its mother feels cold.**

Think of when your mother, or a good friend, insists on making you a cup of tea when you are in a hurry and need to get away quickly. The conversation might go something like this:

You: 'I really have to run now. I'm already late. Sorry I can't stay and visit properly.'

Mother (friend): 'No, don't rush off. I'll make a quick cup of tea and you'll feel much better. Then I won't keep you.'

You: 'That's really kind of you, but no thanks. I don't have time – not even for a quick cup.'

Mother: 'Nonsense. Your trouble is you rush too much. It's not good for you. Now if you just sit down for a minute and have a cup of tea, you will feel much stronger and you will get everything else done that much more efficiently.'

You: 'That's really sweet of you, but it will actually make me more tense because I will be even later than I am now. I really must go right this minute …'

Mother: 'Just look at how pale and exhausted you are. I insist you sit down for a moment and catch your breath. The kettle boiled just now and the water is still hot. It really will take only a minute. I'm not letting you rush off like this – you'll get sick if you don't look after yourself.'

If you have ever had a conversation like that, you will probably be feeling that knot in your stomach while you read it. That knot is part of your response to the *hostility you perceive at an unconscious level*. What is happening is that

Your mother (or your friend) thinks she is being kind and sensitive, but in reality she is neither listening to you nor taking into account your understanding of your own feelings and needs. You feel a victim and are having difficulty staying in control of the situation. In fact, there is very little chance at this stage that you are going to win this battle of wills, unless you become quite firm and take the risk of hurting her feelings.

How much better it would have been if your mother or friend had said:

> Mother: 'Do you have time to stay for a quick cup of tea? I could make it very quickly and it might make you feel much stronger and more able to be efficient.'

> You: 'That's very kind, but I really don't have the time right now. Perhaps I could have tea with you next time I pop in. Would that be okay?'

> Mother: 'I guess you're the best judge of your needs. But I wish you could rest more – I do worry about you!'

There is no tension in that, and no hostility on either side. The difference is, in the second scenario, **your wishes and needs are being taken into account.**

EMPATHY

An attitude is considered empathic when those at the receiving end are allowed to make their own decisions and take responsibility for themselves. The essence of empathy is the ability to understand the other person's point of view. Perhaps the main component of empathy is an acceptance of the fact that *others know more than you do about their own feelings!* Allowing others the freedom to choose and decide (and ask) for themselves is both empathic and warm. The key behaviours here are *asking and listening.*

In order to be empathic, you have to ask questions about how others perceive their situation and how they feel. Then you also have to make a special effort to actually *listen to their reply.* The reply may be entirely different from the one you anticipated!

> Some years ago, my daughter and I had a major burglary in the house we shared. The thieves took a lot of clothing, most of the electrical appliances and several other things. Fortunately we were well insured for the replacement value and our insurance company paid out. Most people, when they heard about the burglary, instantly commiserated with us. 'How dreadful', they said. 'You poor things.'

> *In actual fact, we were rather pleased with the situation. Both of us needed new things and we could not afford to replace the ones we had. I was sick to death of my clothes, and my daughter's radio/tape was not working terribly well. We had enormous fun shopping around for months so that we could get the best bargains and stretch the insurance money to its limits. Not only did we replace what was lost, we were also able to buy the things we needed. And so the burglary had turned out to be to our advantage.*

If our friends had said, 'I hear you had a burglary. How do you feel about it?' we could have told them how pleased we were and they could have rejoiced with us. People's own evaluation of events and their experiences may not be the conventional one.

Similarly, our idea of what is best for others may not coincide with their own idea of what is best for them. We are sometimes far too eager to give what we consider is good advice, or even to tell people what they should do, when it would be so much more helpful to find out first how they feel. Another example of misplaced empathy is the following:

> *A helpful young Boy Scout sees a frail, elderly woman standing at the side of the road, and rushes up to help her across the street. Very kind of him. Except that perhaps she didn't want to go across. Maybe she was waiting to be fetched and needed to stay exactly where she was! What seemed a clear-cut case of need to him might in fact have been altogether different to her.*

It is often much more helpful, and certainly infinitely more sensitive, if we take the trouble first to find out how other people perceive their situation. Empathy is about **consulting**, and **trying to enter into the experience of others**.

 Think, for a moment, of how you listen to other people's news. Do you clarify how they feel about it, or do you tend to make your own value judgement? Try asking more questions; try really listening to people's responses; try to discern the non-verbal message in the tone of voice, the set of the shoulders, the expression on the face. When you find yourself wanting to make friends do what you think is best for them, stop and find out what they consider would be best. You can always have a discussion about it, but until you have consulted them, you really have no right to make suggestions!

JOT DOWN HOW YOU WOULD RESPOND TO A YOUNG PERSON'S SAD TALE OF
LOSING HIS OR HER FIRST JOB:

_____

_____

_____

_____

USING THE FOUR-GROUP DIAGRAM

You may find that your responses during interactions with people generally
fall in one of the four groups of behaviour more often than in the others.
Remember, this does not necessarily mean that you need to apply that label
to yourself as the main truth about yourself, for two reasons. One reason is
that you are always capable of changing. You are constantly making choices
in life and for some reason or another, you have chosen to operate in these
ways. You may at any point decide to choose differently and set about
making that possible. The second reason is that it is quite likely that, within
any interaction, you may well employ up to all four of the styles.

Let's look at them again, this time in more detail.

Group 1: Aggressive controlling behaviours

In the first group, where the behaviours have, to a greater or lesser extent,
the characteristics of being controlling and proactive, I have used the label
'*aggressive controlling*'. In this group we find that people violate the rights of
others by **dominating** them, and by **making decisions on their behalf**
(whether they like it or not).

When people respond or interact in this way, they may be doing it to
cover their own fears and uncertainties; they certainly have a strong need to
control people and situations, and often feel that only by hiding their vul-
nerability will they survive. Many behaviours here are the result of anger,
although on the other hand they are also sometimes the result of thoughtlessness and self-involvement. Sometimes people don't think of what they
are doing and how it will come across, and so they behave in an aggressive,
controlling way without even being conscious of it.

These behaviours may be associated with great business or financial success, but they also have a very high burn-out potential. The price you have
to pay for this kind of behaviour is that you might end up with very few
friends and become a lonely and bitter person. One of the hallmarks of this
group is behaviour that insults, that names, blames and shames others.

Alan was very short, and tried hard to compensate for what he perceived as a shortcoming by behaving in an aggressive way. He prided himself on being a person with whom 'people know where they stand'. He used to declare, 'I don't beat about the bush. I say what is on my mind. If someone upsets me, he is the first to know.'

The trouble was that he upset others rather more than they upset him. He had a disproportionately high turnover of staff in his department. Alan used many naming, blaming and shaming behaviours. He would attack people, calling them names like 'idiot', 'fool', 'incompetent' and a few others we will not print. He would be quick to blame, saying things like, 'Now look what you have done!' or 'It's all your fault. If you had stopped to think, this wouldn't have gone wrong.' He often shouted, and most of the time he began his sentences with 'You …'. He was far too quick to tell people what they should be doing and how they should be doing it. Consequently, he was not a popular man. He came to me because he did not have many friends, and had difficulty in forming and maintaining good relationships.

It took some time for Alan to realise how he sounded, and what he was in fact communicating to other people. When he began to understand that he was behaving aggressively, he realised that people very often respond to aggression in one of two ways: they either run away and hide (in this case, simply to avoid him), or they fight back with equally aggressive behaviour. Either way, a good relationship or friendship is not possible. Before he could put it right Alan had to start listening to the sound of his own words and become conscious of the message he was sending.

If we were to make up a sentence which would typify the attitude underlying aggressive controlling behaviour, it might be, *'I'll decide for you: do it!'*

Aggressive controlling behaviour in the workplace

This is a very common group of behaviours in the workplace. It is common for supervisors to give orders, simply to tell people what to do and how to do it. Even when these orders are pleasantly given, they may come across as controlling and aggressive.

Consider these statements:

- 'Have the completed work on my desk by five o'clock.'
- 'Employees are expected to be at their desks at all times except during designated tea and lunch times.'

- 'Don't bring me problems: bring me solutions.'
- 'Every time you are late for work you will lose one hour's pay.'

You could probably supply any number of similar sentences. In each case, can you see that there is no attempt to allow for discussion, for special circumstances, for difficulties or problems?

WRITE DOWN SOME OF THE THINGS YOU ARE INCLINED TO SAY THAT WOULD FIT INTO THIS CATEGORY:

_____

_____

_____

_____

In each case, the speaker considers only his own requirements, and makes decisions on behalf of others, without consultation. They have no vote, no voice. How much cooperation is there likely to be? In the short term, there may be conformance to the orders, but in the long term, resentment and resistance will grow, loyalty will be lost and, if this is a manager speaking, there will be an increasing gap between manager and workers. Aggressive controlling behaviours are a bad investment in the future.

WRITE DOWN EXAMPLES OF THINGS FITTING INTO THIS CATEGORY THAT ARE SAID TO YOU, AND THINK ABOUT HOW THEY MAKE YOU FEEL:

_____

_____

_____

_____

Now go back to at the previous list (things you are inclined to say) and imagine how your own words affect those who have to listen to them.

Aggressive controlling parenting

Strangely enough, we find many parents whose behaviour fits into this group. They behave in a controlling way towards their children, even when the children have grown up. It makes some sense when your children are small and unable to decide for themselves, although it is possible to be too controlling with even small children and deprive them of the opportunity to develop their own decision-making abilities. Although the lives of small children may depend on their instant acceptance of your command, and immediate obedience to you, aggressive controlling behaviour is hardly appropriate when dealing with adults.

Remember the example of your mother wanting to give you tea when you were in a hurry? Or perhaps she keeps insisting that you have more food because you are 'far too thin'. Or she tells you not to drive alone to the airport at night because it is not safe. All these seemingly kind and loving remonstrations may result in a really negative response from you because of the underlying lack of consultation which constitutes a kind of hostility, a control we instinctively need to resist.

You may be aware of a feeling that she is imposing her will on yours; that she feels she 'knows best' and that, because she means so well, you are unable to tell her to stop. This is what we call a double bind. Whatever you do or say, you will feel guilty.

Other parents continually criticise their children, not because they are not proud of them, but because they want to make them do better or achieve more. Some managers, learning from their home experiences, do the same thing at work, and never give praise in case their staff become 'lazy' or 'complacent'. They continually push them to do better, and when they achieve the goals set, move the goal posts for even better achievements. This need to get others to do what we desire, what we think is right or in their best interest, underlies much of the first group behaviours.

THINK OF SOME OCCASION WHEN YOUR PARENT/TEACHER/EMPLOYER DID NOT GIVEN YOU THE CREDIT YOU DESERVED AND JOT THIS DOWN. DO YOU THINK THEY WERE AFRAID YOU MIGHT HAVE THOUGHT IT WAS NO LONGER NECESSARY TO WORK HARD?

_____

_____

_____

_____

Aggressive controlling behaviour towards friends

We behave in an aggressive controlling way with our friends too. We say, 'What you should do is …' and lay an obligation on them with our understanding of the situation. We interpret things for others, telling them what they should be feeling. We enthuse, 'Oh that's wonderful! You must be so happy!' when perhaps they are not feeling happy at all.

Or we say, 'Relax. Let me help you. I'll do this and this, and you can concentrate on that …' and so we take over. Can you see how this robs people of their right to make their own decisions, and even their own mistakes? The right to make our own decisions and even our own mistakes is one of the most fundamental human rights and we dare not take that away from others.

Furthermore, one of the aspects of being adult is the need (and ability) to take responsibility for our own decisions – to pay the price for our own mistakes. We **disempower** others when we try to impose our advice on them (even if it is obvious *to us* that we are right!).

Delegating

When people behave in a Group I way, delegation becomes a matter of telling others what to do, how to do it and when to do it. To a greater or lesser extent, they will check up on how the job is progressing, and quite often interfere even to the extent of doing part of the job themselves without mentioning the fact. This may lead to confusion and duplication of effort; it will certainly cause frustration and demotivation. True delegation means passing the responsibility, along with the task, to others, and allowing them to exercise as much judgement as the frame of reference negotiated at the beginning will allow.

People inclined towards Group I behaviours wonder why the people they delegate to are so useless and then end up complaining, 'If you want to get something done around here, it is quicker and better to do it yourself.' They claim that they have tried delegating and it didn't work. What really happened, however, is that the mixed messages of, 'Here is a task I will delegate to you because I have confidence in your ability to do it' and 'I can't leave you alone with this task because I am afraid you will mess up' left the person to whom the task was delegated disempowered and frustrated. It wasn't the **delegating** that didn't work, but the Group I way in which it was done that was at fault.

 What does this say about the way we bring up our children? Think back to your own childhood. Can you remember any of the frustrations you felt when you were forced into a course of action against your will? Or given tasks to do and then nagged about them? Are you guilty of doing the same to your children? What might happen if we didn't make our children's decisions for them?

Group 2: Passive manipulating behaviours

I have called the second group of behaviours '*passive manipulating*'. In this group we find behaviours associated with controlling but not taking responsibility. We call this manipulation. You may be at the receiving end of such behaviour quite often. At times you may find yourself doing something you really didn't want to do, but you don't seem to have any tools for getting out of the situation, or any way of making the person stop manipulating you. Ask yourself if you are sometimes guilty of this behaviour yourself.

It's not as if a manipulating person actually tells you what to do. Unlike the first group, behaviour in this group does not rely on open, upfront communication. It never shouts or threatens in so many words. It is difficult to be sure quite what is being said. In fact, manipulation often takes place without any words being spoken at all.

Read my mind …

Some of the most powerful methods of communication in this group (and, sadly, often the most popularly used) are silences and sighs. Underlying this behaviour is an unwillingness to tell others what is really on your mind. Group 2 behaviour comes in the form of hints or indirect suggestions. Those at the receiving end are compelled to play a guessing game, on the basis that, 'if you cared about me you would know …' or 'If you really don't know then I won't tell you' or 'You ought to know …'.

When you communicate in this way, you are trying to do two things: you are attempting to make the other person feel guilty by shifting the responsibility for whatever is going wrong onto that person, and at the same time taking control of the situation while still playing the part of victim or martyr. This may make the recipient feel really dreadful. When such manipulation works well, it can cause tremendous stress, since it makes those at the receiving end feel helpless and confused – is very difficult indeed to win against someone whose behaviour falls in Group 2. People at the receiving end will in all likelihood feel uncomfortable and angry. They may be aware of being controlled or manipulated, but will probably blame themselves and feel that they should have been more intuitive or understanding.

 Do you have a relationship in which you expect your friend or partner or colleague to read your mind? How do you usually handle it when that person fails to get it right? What effect does this have on your relationship?

Blame

One of the most common characteristics of this kind of behaviour is an unwillingness to confront, followed by blame afterwards. The following example will illustrate the pattern:

> Joe: 'Bill makes me so mad when he leaves his papers all over my desk all the time. If he does it again today I am going to throw them out.'
>
> Bob: 'You can't do that! Why don't you rather ask him to put them away? I'm sure he doesn't know it irritates you. He doesn't mean any harm.'
>
> Joe: 'No ways. I won't tell him what to do. He should know better.'
>
> Bob: 'But if it upsets you, tell him.'
>
> Joe: 'No, it wouldn't help. People never consider my feelings.'
>
> Later, when Bill's papers have disappeared and he has finally discovered that Joe threw them away, Joe says, 'Well, it's his own fault. He could see it was irritating me. He should have known …'

These are, of course, not the only type of behaviours in this group.

It won't work

Passive manipulating behaviour often results in a lose-lose situation. It comes across as a kind of blanket sabotage, where anything new is undermined and sabotaged in some way.

Everything is negatively received, although people who act in this way would never dream of speaking up at a meeting or discussion. Only afterwards, will they predict darkly, 'Of course, it won't work.' When others become enthusiastic, they may well warn, 'Just wait and see …' or 'Mark my words – it's only a matter of time …' until everyone is thoroughly demotivated. They often accuse others of being 'naive' and inexperienced.

Of all the strong negative emotions stemming from childhood, perhaps the three most powerful and most enduring are feelings of ignorance, anxiety and guilt. We hate to be made to feel that we are ignorant or naive – it reactivates a time in our lives when others knew everything, we knew nothing and we were very often laughed at. These feelings of inadequacy may bring with them feelings of anxiety and guilt as well.

Such negative behaviours are a variation on the 'Why bother? It won't help' type of behaviour. We encounter this attitude at home as well, where it serves as an excuse for avoiding confrontations and for not resolving issues.

 Think of times when you have been guilty of one of these behaviours. Can you work out why you felt you needed to be so negative? Can you remember hoping that the project would fail so that you would be proved right? Was there something specific you were afraid of?

Dishonesty

Dishonesty is also a hallmark of Group 2 behaviours. It is a very complex behaviour and the reasons for it are equally complex. It is probably enough to understand the underlying patterns. We encounter dishonesty when people avoid the truth or even seem to lie without any real need to. We can understand lying to get out of trouble; we can perhaps understand lying to get out of paying for things; we can even understand lying to appear better than we are. But there are times when many of us find that, for no apparent reason at all, we have not told the truth and we wish we had. We wonder what motivated us.

Naturally, most of the times when we are dishonest, we do not actually lie, but we do manage to be untruthful. We manage to twist the facts, to withhold parts of the information, or appear to be what we are not.

 Think of the times you smile sweetly at someone you despise; or you promise to support someone when you have no real intention of doing so at all. Now think of the times you have been impressed by someone's charming, sympathetic attitude towards you, only to find later that they have been saying dreadful things about you behind your back. Is there a difference between your behaviour and theirs? When is such behaviour justified?

When people behave in this way they generally don't feel good about themselves. They are usually angry and don't believe that others are any good either. Their anger is often deeply hidden; they are merely aware of a feeling that there is nothing to be gained from trying – that the odds are stacked against them, that it won't help to make the effort to be open and honest. Trust in other people is entirely lacking.

They may also have a strong desire to get even, to punish others, although they are careful not to take any risks of confrontation. When people behave in this way they combine a need to control with a victim mentality – not taking responsibility for what happens to them (it is always someone else's fault). Manipulation, deceit, sarcasm and game-playing, as well as emotional blackmail, martyrdom, sulking and hurt-heroism, or cute, clever behaviour and cynicism are all familiar ploys. The right of others to know what they are dealing with, to know the truth, is being violated, although not in as obvious a way as open aggression. The targets of such behaviour may be relatively unaware of what is going on at the time.

The hallmark of this group of behaviours is dishonesty. It involves lying not only to others but also to yourself – and denying your own emotions. This hiding of emotions and misleading of yourself and others can be a breeding ground for suspicion, confusion, frustration and rejection – a sure-fire way of murdering a relationship.

If we were to make a sentence that would typify this group, it could be, 'You decide for me: I'll hate it', perhaps adding, 'And I'll get you for it!' or accompanied by, 'And I won't ever tell you what it was that you did wrong!'

> Imagine it is Friday night. Darling asks, 'What would you like to do – see a movie or go to dinner?'
>
> You reply, 'I don't mind – you choose.' (This is part of the pattern – you want the other person to make the decision so that you do not have to take responsibility for possible failure of the event. Darling must preferably guess that you want to go to dinner and would hate to see a movie.)
>
> 'All right', says Darling, 'let's go to the movies.' 'Very well,' you say through clenched teeth, 'we'll go to a movie.'
>
> 'I can see that's not what you really want,' says Darling, trying hard to get it right. 'Should we rather go to dinner?'
>
> 'No, we'll go to the movies', you insist. Your face is long and hurt, and Darling knows that he or she has guessed wrong. But you will not allow a change now. You are going to make sure that the evening is ruined and thereby punish Darling for being so insensitive.

Does this sound far-fetched? If you observe carefully, you will soon see the pattern in some form or another. You may be at either end of the interaction, but the pattern should be clear. The sad thing is that everyone loses out and nobody is allowed to enjoy the event. No wonder people caught up in these patterns don't stay together.

What lies behind this kind of interaction? Most often, feelings of helplessness; feelings that nothing you can do will make any difference. More often than not, these feelings have their origin in early years, sometimes in childhood when you were powerless to be heard, or perhaps in later years, again when feelings of powerlessness were caused by the people who tried to run your life. Either way, it is essentially an expression of despair.

Group 3: Passive pleasing behaviours

The third group of behaviours is called 'passive pleasing'. You can guess from this label what happens in this group. We behave in this way when we are over-anxious to please and feel uncomfortable with asserting ourselves, our views, or our needs and preferences. Here a combination of warmth and passivity leads to a strong desire to please and a fear of disappointing others. Sadly, this is a common kind of behaviour.

Can't say no

When people behave in this way they feel helpless because they are at the mercy of other people's decisions. They feel that they don't have the right to express their feelings or wants. They are at the mercy of G1 and G2 behaviours. Generally they 'can't say no' and are driven by fear either of being unloved because they are not sufficiently pleasing, or that if they do say no, the person asking will not cope, or will be dreadfully hurt, or will be angry.

They may feel that the whole world depends on them. This attitude is the foundation of what is sometimes called the **compassion trap** (see page 96). For example, a friend asks for a favour, either hinting or saying outright that if you don't comply, she won't be able to cope with her problem, or will be devastated, or in terrible trouble, or very sad, and so on. These powerful, manipulative direct or implied statements are so strong because of the early training many of us have had – that we should always take others into consideration and share all we have. It is very easy for us to be pushed into Group 3 behaviours against our will.

Let's take an example from the office. Staplers and scissors seem to be articles that most often disappear in offices, so many people simply refuse to lend theirs to anyone at all. Are you able to say no when someone asks you for yours? If you find that, although you have decided not to lend them to anyone, you are still unable to refuse when someone asks nicely, then your behaviour falls in G3. The trouble is that, although you feel you are being kind and obliging when you give in, you are probably going to be resentful and angry with the person you obliged when you need the article and it has not been returned. *G3 behaviours seem a good idea at the time, but very often lead to overload, stress and resentment.*

THINK OF A SITUATION IN WHICH YOU FIND IT PARTICULARLY DIFFICULT TO SAY NO. WHAT MAKES IT SO HARD?

_____

_____

_____

_____

_____

Against your will

It is important to understand that there is a difference between doing things for others and saying yes as a result of **your own decision** (a good and friendly thing to do), and doing things for others **against your better judgement** because you can't say no (sometimes a disaster). It is fine to say yes to all kinds of requests if you want to, but if you say yes simply because you cannot say no, your behaviour is the G3 kind and you are allowing others to run your life by their demands – being a victim of their needs and agendas.

You can probably identify colleagues at your workplace who can't say no. They are the ones who always cover for everyone else, who work overtime without pay, who fetch and carry for others, who end up undertaking all the tasks others don't want to do. They may even be laughed at behind their backs. I am sure you have heard something like, 'Ask Mary-Jo – she always says yes. She's a sucker for punishment!'

A sentence to typify behaviours in the passive pleasing group could be, *'You decide for me: I'll do it!* I might not like it, but I will do it anyway, especially if you put pressure on me or ask me over and over again. How could I bear to refuse?'

People inclined towards this kind of behaviour often lay guilt trips on the very people they so lovingly serve by always saying yes, whatever the cost. People who care might even become reluctant to ask for favours because they know the answer will be yes, even if it is not at all convenient.

Listen to the story of Kim. She couldn't refuse anyone who needed help.

I asked Kim one day if she intended going to town in the morning – I simply had to get my tax return in by the due date. She replied, 'Yes, I can go to town.'

'But are you going anyway?' I asked.

'Why?'

'Well I need to drop off my tax return, and I would rather not make a special trip if someone is going anyway.'

'I'd be happy to drop it off for you,' she said.

It was only later that I discovered that she had gone to enormous trouble to rearrange her schedule for the following day so that she was able to make a special trip into town to drop off my return. I felt uncomfortable about it and wished she had been more honest. In fact, after several similar incidents, I stopped asking her for anything in case she said yes and it was inconvenient. I didn't want to carry the guilt of disrupting her life. Far from doing me a favour, she actually deprived me of the freedom to ask her and to conduct an open and equal friendship.

While people inclined towards this group of behaviours undoubtedly wallow in much attention, sympathy, appreciation and protection, they pay for it with their loss of freedom, self-respect and creativity. They are often fearful, driven by a need to be well thought-of and a great fear of being unloved. They frequently don't really know who they are or what they think because they have never expressed and acted upon their own opinions or risked making their own requests.

Victims and bad influences

Behaviours in this group are often responsible for the downfall of people who 'get into bad company'. These behaviours may result in those indulging in them being the ones who get caught, because they were drawn into a situation against their will. They are the ones who are abused and do not fight back because they 'don't want to get others into trouble' or 'don't want to create a scene'. These are the girls who get pregnant as a result of a date rape and never tell who the father is. These are the boys who take the rap for the dagga they didn't smoke and that didn't belong to them. These are the people who are late for their own weddings because someone needed a lift somewhere. They are the subjects of many sitcoms, and although the situations they land themselves in may well be comic to an extent, they are far more often tragic.

People whose dominant behaviours fall into G3 become so entrapped by their concern for others that they are unable to lead their own lives. They are no longer able, most of the time, **to make their own decisions**, and very often they completely lose touch with their own feelings, their own likes and dislikes. This is a high price to pay for pleasing people, and is a very poor investment in the future.

Group 4: Free responsible behaviours

The fourth group of behaviours is called 'free responsible', because the behaviours in this quadrant are free (not controlled by anyone else), but at the same time responsible (they allow others the same freedom). But responsibility towards others does not mean requiring them to be as assertive or free as ourselves. It takes into consideration the feelings and opinions of others. The sentence we could use to typify this group's behaviours might be, 'I'll decide for me: you decide for you, if you want to'.

This attitude involves conferring with others, really listening to them and considering their feelings and needs. When we reach the point where we decide for others that they should take responsibility for themselves, and try to make that happen, we have crossed over into G1 and are trying to control!

APPLICATION

The differences between the groups become very clear when we take something simple, such as a suggestion to go for a walk, and see how that may typically be dealt with in any one group.

In G1, Mary may say briskly, 'Come for a walk – it will be good for you!' or 'Come along, we're all going for a walk.' In both these cases, can you see how Mary has made a decision for everybody? And how there is a definite element of control in it? This may be kindly meant, but it is still not allowing others to make up their own minds, nor is it considering the feelings or wants of the others.

In the second group, Jack may lament, 'No-one ever comes walking with me. I suppose I'll just have to go alone as usual.' Or, when it is too late to go, 'I really wanted to go for a walk today …' Can you see how this closes the door to constructive interaction? Even if Jim says, 'I'll come with you' or 'Oh, I'm sorry – I didn't know you wanted to go out,' Jack may say sarcastically, 'Oh, don't bother, I'm used to it!' or 'Please don't put yourself to any trouble on my account.' Whatever happens, there will be an atmosphere of nastiness and everyone will be the loser.

In the third group, Peter is likely to test the wishes of Larry and let that be the deciding factor. 'Do you want to go for a walk?' If Larry says yes, the walk is on. If he says no, the walk is off. This puts rather a lot of responsibility on Larry, while Peter takes no responsibility at all for his own pleasure – if he gets no exercise, he has someone to blame for it!

In G4, Jill might announce, 'I'm going for a walk. Would you like to come with me?' If Hilary says yes, well and good. If Hilary says no, Jill goes alone. Either way both get to take responsibility for their own actions and well-being and both can do what they would prefer with their time. Naturally, that does not mean that the person who asked may not be disappointed if the other would prefer to stay home. But it does mean that no-one need feel resentful or made to do something against their will.

You can see how much more pleasant life would be if we were all as honest about what we wanted and intended to do as Jill using G4 behaviour, while at the same time allowing others space to do the same.

The four behaviour groups relate roughly to the following labels you may be more familiar with:.

Group 1: Aggression

Bearing in mind that the cornerstone of aggression is an unwillingness (or inability) to consider other people's point of view, then Group 1 is very similar to the Aggressive category normally used in Assertiveness classification. Aggression leads to a win-lose situation.

Group 2: Indirect aggression

The hallmarks of dishonesty, hidden anger, sulking, sarcasm and a desire to control without taking responsibility are all here. It is often difficult to put your finger on exactly why you are uncomfortable with someone who is using this group of behaviours. Indirect aggression leads to a lose-lose situation.

Group 3: Submission

While submission is a comfortable way to have people around you behaving (especially those working for you), in the long term it does not work well. There is a high degree of burn-out, and people are unable to grow and develop. They may never get in touch with who they really are, and the fullness of their personality and abilities will be denied. Submission leads to a lose-win situation.

Group 4: Assertiveness

In this group, the combination of being proactive (decisive) and warm leads to an acknowledgement of the rights of others without a loss of your own. It allows others to make their own decisions with responsibility, to choose to take risks or grow through pain without blaming anyone else. It allows others to make up their own minds, even if it means allowing them to make their own mistakes. The hallmark of behaviours in this group is honesty. Since people know where they stand, they tend to respond with respect, love, support and acceptance. This is a powerful and empowering group, and people behaving in G4 tend to end up with good friends, the respect and gratitude of others, and peace of mind. They do not allow themselves to be manipulated. This leads to a win-win situation.

Identifying and changing our dominant behaviours

The important thing to remember is that none of us *lives* in any group. None of us always behaves in any one way. We tend to visit all the groups sooner or later, although we may spend most of our time in one or another of them.

TAKE A MOMENT TO IDENTIFY YOUR DOMINANT GROUP OF BEHAVIOURS, WRITE THIS DOWN AND DECIDE IF THAT IS THE WAY YOU WANT TO BEHAVE:

_____

_____

_____

_____

If this is not the way you want to behave, set about working out how you intend changing. Some suggestions follow.

From G1 to G4

What separates G1 from G4 behaviours is how much consideration you show for the right of others to make up their own minds. If your G1 behaviours are just a habit you have fallen into, and arise from thoughtlessness, simply because you never realised that you were behaving in this way, you will not find it difficult to begin consulting other people's opinions and feelings. In fact, you will probably find you enjoy it and are constantly surprised at the variety and maturity of people's responses. (The opposite is also possible, unfortunately!)

But if you have a temper that refuses to stay under control, or you find that you are constantly angry, there may well be more to your behaviour than meets the eye. I often find that people who behave aggressively are hiding deep wounds, or feel unsafe in some way or another. This may be true in your case, and it is certainly not your fault at all. There is no blame to be apportioned for feeling that way. But constantly behaving aggressively is a matter of choice: *you can do something about it*, and it would be a good idea to obtain some counselling so that you can deal with your underlying problem. While we cannot be blamed for the scars we carry from our past, we certainly are responsible for what we do with them, and the good news is that **we can change**.

Imagine how it would feel to be free to be gentle and polite to others, and find that their response to you is pleasant, cooperative and loving.

Getting out of G2
If you discover that you are behaving in Group 2, perhaps by objecting to something your boss has said or done, but behind her back instead of to her face, try the following to get out of that quadrant:

■ Take responsibility for what you are feeling and acknowledge that these are your own feelings and that you can **choose** to feel that way or not.
■ Be more honest about what you are feeling and saying; go back to your boss and tell her how you feel. This may, of course, be a 'career-limiting move', if your boss doesn't take well to negative feedback. On the other hand, it may be worth the risk, since the alternative is to set up a far more damaging pattern by holding your anger inside. This is a pattern that may eventually destroy both you and your job. You may decide that it is better to take the risk of incurring your boss's anger than to live with the certainty that G2 behaviour is damaging.

Moving from G3 to G4
Similarly, if you find yourself in Group 3, all you need to do to get out of that quadrant and into G4 is to take responsibility for your own decision, say politely and firmly what you have decided, and stick to it.

We will be looking at specific ways of changing your dominant behaviours in the chapters that follow.

> **The important thing is to remember
> that it is never too late to change.**

CHAPTER 3

When Adult Meets Adult

*At every single moment of one's life one is what one is going to be
no less than what one has been.*
OSCAR WILDE

Have you ever been surprised or irritated with yourself about the way you reacted to something someone said or did? Perhaps you muttered at yourself afterwards and wished you had handled it quite differently. But when a similar situation arose, you reacted the same way. The secret of this **behaviour pattern** may lie in understanding the Transactional Analysis theory of behaviour – it is certainly very revealing.

EGO STATES

Some years ago, Dr Eric Berne developed a theory for understanding human behaviours which he called Transactional Analysis (TA). This theory is based on our responses and reactions to one another, what could be called the transaction between people. He identified three ego states, or aspects of ourselves, which he called the *Parent*, the *Adult* and the *Child*.

We may be said to act, feel and think from a position based on these different ego states. It is from these positions that we respond to various events in our lives, and the information in each ego state is responsible for our sometimes rational, sometimes irrational responses and reactions to people, situations and events. All of us, at any age, can act in any one of these states. Both the causes and the effects of these different ways of interacting are complex. In this book we will not go into this in any detail. We will do no more than use one tiny corner of the theory – we will explore what forms the basis of each ego state and therefore what 'drives' us in each, as this affects the way in which we communicate.

Child

This is the earliest of our ego states but it remains part of us to our dying day. It does not deal in facts or judgements, but is dominated by feelings. When our 'feelings run away with us' and we respond emotionally rather than rationally, we are responding in the Child ego state. This does not imply that we are being childish; it is more a state of being **childlike**. The Child ego state has its roots in our earliest years, even before birth, before we could think and reason rationally.

Parent

This ego state has nothing to do with having children yourself. It starts developing before you are a year old and is a bit like an ever-running tape recorder. It refers to the sum total of all the significant input we have received through our childhood and formative years. There are generally two main inner 'voices' or patterns. These voices or patterns are initially from our mother and from our father (or from our primary caregivers) and they are the source of a vast amount of information on values, morals, standards, conventions, as well as the view we have of ourselves, other people and life in general. Other adults, whose opinions and information we were obliged to accept, such as teachers, grandparents, and so on, also contribute to the content of our Parent state. From these and other sources we derive the 'should', 'must', 'good', and 'the right way' rules, which collectively are responsible for all our prejudices, as well as our feelings of anxiety, ignorance and guilt.

As we grow older, we collect more 'recordings' in our Parent ego state – from our peers, our colleagues, and our family. These 'recordings' are the basis for our prejudices as well as for our standards, and we often use them to lay down the law. **A prejudice is anything that is pre-judged – decided or accepted without examination.** Much of the language in our Parent state may be very dominant and commanding, echoing what we gathered along the way.

> **Our prejudices are like physical infirmities – we cannot do what they prevent us from doing.**
> JOHN LANCASTER SPALDING

Adult

In this ego state we gather our own empirical information and evaluate both Child and Parent. In our Adult state we tend to be rational, sensible and useful, unprejudiced and able to respond to other people's needs. It is the most useful ego state and the one we would wish to dominate our lives from day to day. In this state we keep asking, 'Is that right? Do I really think that?'

PARENTAL MESSAGES

Let's discover some of the information in our Parent 'recordings'.

Memories from our childhood are sometimes rather strange ones, and fun! I remember discovering about built-in cupboards one Sunday afternoon in Kimberley. My grandfather was taking us for a walk while our parents rested, and we wandered through a building site across the road. He told us that they were building flats. That bothered me, because in my three-year-old mind, building involved going up, and flat was definitely all on one plane!

In the foundations we found some tiny rooms and I asked what they were. Grandpa said they were the foundations for the built-in cupboards. 'What are built-in cupboards?' I asked. His reply enchanted me. 'There's a wall,' he said, 'with a door in it, and inside the door is a wardrobe.' How mysterious and exciting that seemed!

 What can you remember about your childhood? Don't worry if you can't recall anything from before you entered school – many people have very dim memories of their early days.

Think back to your childhood. Can you remember anything from when you were quite tiny? Can you, for instance, remember where you used to play? Or who you played with? Did you have a favourite toy? Or a favourite relative? Sometimes all we can remember are little pictures of individual events, some nice, some horrible.

WRITE DOWN SOME OF YOUR CHILDHOOD MEMORIES:

_____

_____

_____

_____

_____

What were the things that significant people said to you? Do you remember fairly insignificant things like, 'Eat your cabbage!' or more judgemental remarks such as, 'Nice people don't do that.'?

Sometimes things that significant people in our lives say to us stay with us for a very long time and affect our self-image and the way in which we behave towards others.

> I can remember hearing my elder sister and my mother discussing me when I was about eight or nine years old. I overheard my sister exclaim, 'It doesn't matter what we put her in, she always looks dreadful!' I was certainly not a proud mother's idea of a dress-conscious little girl, but that remark stayed with me and made it difficult for me to shop for clothes for another 40 years. I knew I would look awful whatever I wore.

NOW SEE IF YOU CAN CATCH SOME OF THE VOICES OF YOUR CHILDHOOD AND WRITE DOWN SOME OF THE THINGS YOU REMEMBER BEING TOLD:

_____

_____

_____

_____

_____

Useful messages versus harmful messages

These memories are some of the 'recordings' that are in our Parent ego state. They form the basis for all our value systems, for our ideas on how things should be done (like how to tie a bow, or how to hold our knife and fork), and account to a large degree for our ideas of who we are and where we fit into society. These messages come not only from our parents, but from all significant people in our lives over the years. There are probably quite a number of messages about ourselves too. For example: 'You're so clumsy!' or 'What a clever child you are!' or 'Why can't you ever do anything right?' and so on. Some of these voices will be complimentary and some of them quite the opposite. Many of us who battle with insecurities and a poor self-image are bound by messages in our Parent ego state, and we will not be able to free ourselves from them before we have identified them. Then we have to work towards replacing them with true evaluations.

Some of these messages from our childhood may also prevent us from interacting well with other people, particularly in the workplace. If we have been taught that we are not as good as other people, effective communication and confident teamwork will be very difficult for us. If we have been told that we are inadequate, or will never succeed, we will find it very difficult to get anywhere, and will probably spend a great deal of our time desperately trying to please others (Group 3 behaviour, see page 43). If we have been taught that we are better than others, we will also find it difficult to get on with others on an equal footing!

If we have been taught that we are victims, and that we must not *openly* stand up for our rights, that we must simply accept what comes our way because we have no rights and no right to resist openly, we will find that our behaviour fits into Group 2 most of the time.

 You might like to spend some time on this: it will certainly be time well spent. If you can identify what you hidden messages are, and how they tend to determine what you feel and what you do, you will have gone a long way towards being able to change the ones you are not happy to keep. Go back to the 'I remember being told' exercise and fill in more messages as they occur to you. They may be quite an eye-opener!

You may prefer to engage the services of a psychologist, who is trained to help you identify these messages and evaluate them. Psychological help will enable you to exchange your identified messages for new messages that empower and liberate you.

If you prefer to work on your own, keep asking yourself, 'Why do I think that?' or 'Who told me that that is so?' and then decide if you agree. This evaluation of inherited values will be, at the very least, interesting. At best, you may find yourself able to rid yourself of those that are mere prejudice and cherish the ones that seem to fit the facts as you see them now.

Consider this example: Think about the message which many of us have received, that 'people who eat with their mouths open are not nice'. If you investigate that 'truism', you will find that there are many really nice people who have the unfortunate habit of eating with their mouths open, and as many horrible people who eat with their mouths closed! Should you keep this judgement as it is, or should it be modified?

WRITE A NEW VERSION OF THIS MESSAGE (OR ANY SIMILAR MESSAGE) WHICH YOU FEEL MAY BE MORE ACCURATE AND FACTUAL:

_____

_____

_____

_____

Continue your own evaluation of inherited values and hidden messages in your Parent state in the same way. Think especially of the messages you hold concerning yourself and decide whether they are true or false. You may find you are nicer than you feared!

> **Freedom means
> choosing your own burden.**
> HEPHZIBAH MENUHIN

CHAPTER 4

What we Think – How we Feel

*Misunderstanding may occur
not only through wrong or excessive expression of feeling,
but through repression and failure to express ...*
CHARLES W VALENTINE

Free, responsible communication is about taking full responsibility for the way you feel and the way you behave. It is about allowing others to take full responsibility for themselves. It is an Adult-Adult communication which not only has the best chance of being the most effective form of communication, but is also responsible for far less wear and tear on you!

TAKING RESPONSIBILITY

Behaving responsibly means that you have a certain amount of **control** over yourself. It does not have to be complete control, but enough to enable you to choose to behave in a way which will help you get your message across. We often refer to this taking responsibility for ourselves and our own well-being as assertiveness, and certainly being assertive is very attractive. But we should never confuse assertiveness with aggression, which is hostile.

In the previous chapter, we looked at the way we collect messages from our parents and other significant people, and how these provide us with the basis on which we make judgements. Discovering what is recorded in our Parent ego state is an important step towards being able to evaluate the messages for ourselves and to make our own choices in adult life.

You may find it hard to exercise your choices and, therefore, to act assertively. This can be made even more difficult if you experience feelings of insecurity, or certain other emotions, especially when they are extreme. These problem feelings are:

- Excessive anger
- Excessive anxiety
- Uncontrolled depression.

Note that anger, anxiety and feelings of depression are perfectly normal and healthy. It is only when these emotions become extreme or uncontrolled that they cause problems.

When you are excessively angry, you are likely to express that anger in aggressive behaviour. If you are excessively anxious, you are likely to behave in a non-assertive, submissive way. When you are feeling really depressed, it is difficult to express yourself at all.

EMOTIONS JUST HAPPEN

There is no way in the world that we can stop our emotions from happening and absolutely no reason why we should. It is quite useless to try to turn emotions on and off: if you were to decide right now that you want to feel elated, for argument's sake, or deeply distressed, you would probably not be able to manufacture that feeling without a situation that generated that response in you. That is because our emotions are the medium through which we respond to situations that arise in our lives.

The problem is not that we are emotional, but that our emotions sometimes take control of us, and drive us to act in ways we would prefer not to, and may regret later. So we need to find a way to moderate these emotions, while still giving ourselves permission to experience them.

> **People are disturbed not by things
> but by the view they take of them.**
> MARCUS AURELIUS

One method of working towards gaining control over the degree of these feelings is to examine the rationality behind what we are saying to ourselves in any situation. This is because what we feel is, to a large extent, the direct result of what we tell ourselves.

Think about why it is that the same event, experienced by two or three different people, may **elicit** two or three completely **different responses**. One person may be furious, another unperturbed, and yet another mildly irritated. In each case, the emotional response is determined by the **expectations** that person has of life and of people. The person who is furious may be so because she believes that whatever happened should never have happened like that. In her mind she is saying something to this effect: 'This is ridiculous! They shouldn't behave like that! They have no right! I don't have to put up with this!' The other two would have been saying quite different things in their minds, probably being a lot more understanding, compassionate and rational.

SELF-TALK

We call these beliefs or expectations and the way we talk to ourselves 'self-talk'. Take this example, for instance:

> *You walk down a dark alleyway late at night, and see the shadowy shape of a person walking towards you in the half-light. How do you feel? Probably nervous. Why? Because you have been taught not to go down dark alleyways alone at night because they are dangerous. So you are probably saying something along the lines of, 'I am in a dangerous situation. Something terrible may happen at any moment. This dark shadowy person may turn out to be someone who wants to kill or maim me…'. It is natural that you should be feeling scared. Fear is an appropriate feeling in the circumstances.*

> *But what if that same dark alleyway is familiar, perhaps near your home, and the shadowy figure is calling your name and is someone you trust coming towards you to welcome you home? You would feel different. Same alleyway, same dark night, same shadowy figure, but different messages. You would then be saying to yourself, 'I am safe now. Thank goodness this is someone I love and who cares about me.'*

Catching your self-talk

Notice what goes on in your head when someone near you in the traffic suddenly changes lanes and drives in a way that you perceive to be irresponsible. The more you think nasty things about the driver, the angrier you become. The more you 'feed' your anger with interpretations of what the driver may have intended, what he may be like at home, whether or not he bought his licence, and even whether he is unkind to animals, the more upset you will become.

If, on the other hand, you think about the times you have made an error of judgement in traffic, or not seen someone until it was nearly too late, you may find yourself not upset at all about the other person's driving, but relieved that no damage was done. Then, instead of saying, 'The idiot! Why doesn't he look where he's going? Typical BMW/taxi driver!' or whatever, you may be saying, 'Poor thing, he must have got an awful fright,' and feel quite sympathetic instead. If that response seems far-fetched, try it! You may find that driving becomes a lot less stressful.

So we could ask ourselves the question, 'Why do I feel the way I do? What are the messages I am giving myself?'

To find these messages, we have to work backwards. We have to discover what the filter is (see page 24) that we are using to interpret situations. Let's look at an example.

> *Imagine it is three o'clock in the morning in the middle of winter and you are standing on a lonely station platform in the middle of nowhere. How do you feel? You might feel lonely, deserted, frightened, angry, anxious, miserable or put upon because you have been asked to fetch someone from the station at this ungodly hour. Unless it is your beloved, that is, in which case you may well be feeling excited, alive, full of anticipation and happy. The situation is the same. None of the external factors has changed. What is different is what you are saying to yourself.*
>
> *Instead of 'Poor me', you are saying, 'I can't wait!' Instead of saying, 'I'm always the one who has to do all the dirty work around here. It's not fair. Nobody cares about my welfare or how I feel,' you are telling yourself, 'I'm so happy. I'm really glad I managed to come alone to fetch her – we can have some time together alone on the way home. This is the best night of my life.'*

The only difference between feeling awful and feeling great is what you tell yourself about the situation. The emotion you feel is governed by your interpretation of the situation, and that is the result of the things you tell yourself. This is hardly a new idea.

The famous Frenchman, Descartes, said, 'I think, therefore I am.' Marcus Aurelius, the Roman emperor, remarked, 'People are disturbed not by things but by the view they take of them.' His idea was that we define who we are by what we think. In other words, as Shakespeare said, 'Nothing is as it seems, but thinking makes it so.'

Certainly, the filter through which we perceive matters influences how we feel, and how we feel greatly influences how we behave and who we are.

Sometimes our filters are such that they make us produce excessive emotions in response to situations. These filters may be major factors in producing in us behaviours that are not helpful and that we should rather avoid.

The principle of examining our self-talk may be used to deal with feelings in order to place them under firmer, more conscious control. It is not the event or happening which causes us to feel angry, hurt, sad or happy, but what we think about it, what we say to ourselves to interpret it. Let's see how we can identify these interpretations, these filters.

Irrational self-talk

Self-talk can be rational or irrational. Rational ideas are true and bear a firm relation to fact. Rational ideas are not demanding, unrealistic or exaggerated. Our responses are appropriate to the reality of the situation.

Irrational ideas are untrue (although there is often a grain of truth in them). From irrational ideas we tend to draw invalid conclusions founded on beliefs we have inherited or developed, without testing them against reality. A good label for such irrational conclusions is 'misbelief', a term coined by William Backus and Marie Chapian in their helpful book *Telling yourself the Truth*. I think this term describes irrational self-talk pretty well.

Irrational thought, or misbelief, often makes no allowances for the failure of others or ourselves, and the subsequent response is therefore inappropriate. Some of the more common pitfalls of irrational thinking involve making assumptions that *demand* that life be a particular way. Some of us genuinely think that life should treat us kindly, that if things go wrong, we have a *right* to complain.

Expectations

Frequently, we are very angry when people do not behave in a way we consider right or moral. The sort of words that warn us about this kind of thinking include 'should', 'must', 'ought', and their negatives. Is it a realistic expectation to want everyone to behave the way we consider the right way? Think about what would happen if everyone had to behave as everyone else thought they should. It is simply not possible, is it? What gives us the idea that our values and judgements are the ones the world should adopt? It is unrealistic to expect the world to run to our own advantage, or to hope that other people will behave according to our standards. Why should they?

Your values are generally **inherited** from your parents or primary caregivers within your cultural group. Other people were not raised by the same people as you were, and it is more than likely that they were taught a set of values in some ways different from your own. Who decides which set of values is the correct and only one?

We may get caught up in **catastrophising** – a lovely word describing the tendency to make things out to be disasters when they are in fact mere inconveniences. We may use phrases such as, 'This is too much – I can't cope!' or 'What a disaster!' Or we may draw exaggerated conclusions from isolated events. We may groan, 'I'm a failure – I will never get anything right!' or exclaim, 'You never do anything right!' when the smallest things go wrong.

> *At a dinner party, perhaps the hostess discovers that two of her guests were lovers some while back, and had parted on bad terms. When she tells her friend about it the next day, she exclaims 'It was an absolute disaster! I was so embarrassed I wanted to die!' Obviously it was not really a disaster, merely a social gaffe causing a few hours of difficult socialising. When history is written it is unlikely this dinner party will be mentioned in the Disasters of our Time list!*

It is sometimes fun to exaggerate simply for effect, but when we keep using these extreme, catastrophic words in connection with our own experiences, we may well begin to believe them and build up a sense of outrage that life could be so bad.

A really tricky kind of thinking sees no grey areas in life, preferring to have things **either right or wrong**. So you may be a dearest friend until you do one thing not appreciated, whereupon you become an enemy; or a situation will be judged to be either wonderful or disastrous, with no grades of value in between. Such thinking leads to a great deal of emotional stress.

Inherited messages in irrational self-talk

Some common recorded messages in your Parent state that contribute to irrational thinking and therefore make free, responsible communication difficult when they are not challenged, are:

■ *I must do well. People must always think well of me. If I don't bring glory to the family name, I will bring shame.*
Such self-talk brings about an irrational fear of failure, and you may experience tremendous guilt if you are not an outstanding achiever, or if you are passed over for promotion.

■ *It is unforgivable to make a mistake. If something is worth doing, it is worth doing well (or not at all!).*
Being a perfectionist leaves you open to a great deal of unnecessary stress. It is quite all right to make mistakes, and even to do things badly, just as

long as they get done, or you have done your best. One very successful American company states 'If you are not making mistakes, you are not doing enough work!'

■ *I must always put others before myself – I am only here for the benefit of others.*
This apparently altruistic thought is actually bad management of your own resources. If you wish to be effective and successful (and therefore able to help others), you will need to look after yourself, give yourself time off, discover and express your own opinions and preferences, and see that you reach your full potential.

■ *People who do wrong things should be punished/should be excluded from society. (Therefore I dare not go wrong.)*
We all do wrong things sooner or later. If this is one of your messages, you will have a powerful need to hide, to cover up, to lie. You will be desperately afraid of being found out and therefore punished. Most wrong things can easily be put right and that can be the end of it.

■ *I must at all cost know what is up ahead so that I can plan for it: it is impossible to live with uncertainties.*
It is absolutely not necessary to try to control everything, so you really do not need to know what lies in the future. A certain amount of information helps you plan and make provision for the future, but flexibility and an ability to enjoy surprises will stand you in far better stead.

■ *History always repeats itself/you can't escape from your past.*
You certainly can escape from your past, if you put your mind to it. Nobody needs to be bound by the past, either by what you have done yourself, or by what has been done to you. Move on and prove that life is what you make of it.

■ *It's no use even trying because I am what I am – a failure like my dad/mom/ grandparents/sister/brother.*
Giving up, putting the blame on others and refusing to take responsibility for who you are and what you do all prevent you from G4 behaviour and lock you into G2 behaviour – the most destructive group of behaviours. Whatever negative things you have been told, you **can** change, and it is **never** too late!

■ *It's no use even trying because I never get a fair deal. It's because of my colour/because I'm poor/because I live in the country/because I'm a foreigner.*
This self-talk closely resembles the 'I am what I am' kind and may be the

result of similar messages you heard from others thinking like you. Choosing to hold on to this self-talk will ensure that you never get promotion, not because of what you have suggested, but because your attitude is so negative. People with a positive, confident attitude, who behave in a free, responsible manner, have a much better chance of achieving their goals.

Rational self-talk

Rational thinking is based on reality and is supported by the facts. Rational thinking is not merely based on our own assumptions. It lacks the demanding nature of irrational thought and accepts that it is all right for the world to be the way it is for the moment, that others are free to behave in the way they see fit, and that each is allowed to be human. Rational thoughts foster emotions that are manageable and appropriate. Because it deals with events and people as they in fact are, rational thought is the most effective way of processing events and leads to good and happy interactions with other people. It resists manipulation by challenging the fundamental rules.

CHECK YOUR THINKING AND SELF-TALK

When examining our self-talk we need to ask ourselves these questions:

- Why should things be the way I want them to be? Am I turning my preference into a standard for everyone?
- What makes me so special that only good things should happen to me? What is unfair about having my share of the unpleasantness in the world?
- What makes me think that I'm so influential that I'm responsible for everyone else's well-being, and that others will not cope if I make a mistake?
- What makes me think that someone else has the right to set my standards and make my decisions for me?

How others see us

It is usually not difficult to identify our self-talk because we so often actually 'speak' to or lecture ourselves. I am sure that you have also, when you have done something particularly stupid, said to yourself, 'You idiot!' or 'Here you go again!' It is not good for you to hear your own voice putting yourself down even in a joke. Make sure that the things you say to yourself are in fact true, and generally **supportive**. Your evaluation of yourself has a tremendous effect both on the way you are and on the way other people see you and respond to you.

In fact, if you find that others often treat you like an idiot, or as if you are a weak person who cannot cope with circumstances that come your way so that you need to be protected from all reality, perhaps it will be worthwhile examining what sort of labels you are giving yourself. Those labels will affect your estimation of yourself, and that, in turn, will communicate itself to others so that they have an idea of how you expect to be treated!

Try this experiment with some close friends or family you can trust to be honest with you. Ask them if they will observe you while you do this. Explain that you will be walking in and out of the room three times without saying anything. Their task is not to guess anything, but to *concentrate on their response to you* – how they *feel* towards you. They don't have to work out what you are doing. They just have to get in touch with their own feelings about you. Then walk out of the room and spend a few moments getting as clear a picture of yourself in relation to them as you can.

First think along these lines: 'I am not much good at anything. They probably secretly think I am wasting their time. I hope they are not saying nasty things about me while I am out here …' Then walk in, smile at them if you can and sit down, all the time thinking about how useless you are. Then go out again. Don't discuss it yet.

This time, think along these lines: 'What a wonderful person I am! I can't think why I waste my time with these poor, insignificant, stupid people. They're lucky I'm so kind to them. I expect they will be wasting more of my time when I go back in. Still, I will put up with it out of the goodness of my generous heart …' Then walk back in, smile and sit down. You may find that you feel different and walk differently. I am sure your smile looks different. Then go out again. Don't discuss it yet.

The third time, think along these lines: 'This is fun. They're nice and so am I. We're fortunate to have such a good relationship and I imagine they're having as much fun trying this out as I am. I know they love me because I am lovable, and I love them because they are too …' Then go in, smile and sit down.

Now ask them which one of you they preferred. Which one did they feel warm towards? Which one would they choose as a friend? Which one would they tend to be pleasant to? You will probably find, if your thoughts were clear enough, that they will choose the third.

If you ask them how they felt towards the other two, you will probably find that they did not much like them, the first one because you did not like yourself, and the second because you found it necessary to consider yourself much better than you were – strangely enough, another form of self-hate. In all three cases, the picture you had of yourself greatly influenced the picture *they* received of you and how *they* felt towards you. The pictures you have of yourself affect the way people respond to you in an immediate and powerful way.

Similarly, how people respond to you and what they say to you may have an equally powerful effect on the way you see yourself, unless you decide to be selective about what you believe of other people's opinions of you. While you're working on your positive, cheerful and lovable picture of yourself, there may be those who are putting you down. What can you do about this?

Dealing with negative friends and colleagues

If you find that friends or colleagues persist in treating you in a negative way, mention to them that you feel differently about yourself, if you can. You could try telling them, 'I'm sorry you see me like that – I feel so much better about myself these days and I think I am really changing' or something along those lines. If they persist with negatives, spend less time with them if you can and try to understand that their opinions come from their view of the world. They are seeing you through the *filters of their own minds* and these may be speckled with sad experiences.

 Remember that our mental 'filters' are made up of all the experiences and memories we have collected over the years, and some are very jaundiced, while others are really rather pleasant. Remember what we said about evaluating the messages from the past? We have ownership of what makes up our own filters as well, and with some effort, we can learn to see things differently, to interpret experiences more enjoyably ,and subsequently we can become more positive all round.

But bear in mind not everyone is on the same learning curve, and you may have to deal with people who are stuck in their negative patterns. Be kind to them, but don't allow their sadness to discolour your view of yourself as you grow in confidence and strength.

THINK AGAIN

The self-talk going on inside your head in relation to events and to yourself has a powerful effect on who you are. Therefore you need to *examine these messages well* and become continually *aware of what is happening in your mind.* What follows is a suggestion of how you could approach doing that.

Dealing with irrational self-talk

Our aim here is to develop a belief system or filter that is made up of true, appropriate and positive self-talk instead of the often problematic self-talk we may now have. To analyse our self-talk, we have to look at the entire process:

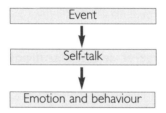

In other words, an event takes place, followed by our self-talk, which in turn prompts our response to the event — our emotions and our behaviour.

But you may be unaware of the self-talk that is being brought into play — sometimes things happen so fast that you are quite certain that there has been no time for self-talk at all. In fact, a great deal of the process will be contained in your Parent ego state, all worked out for you. All that is required for your automatic response to emerge is a key word or experience.

To begin with, you will probably find that you are unaware of how your sudden, instinctive emotions came to the fore. If you make a conscious effort you can begin to listen to yourself so that you gradually become aware of what you are telling yourself. But it will not be enough merely to be aware of the self-talk: you will also have to learn to challenge it.

Let's use an example to explain how the process works:

Event: *Your friend Bob did something which you thought was nasty.*
Emotion: *You felt excessively angry with him. You spent several days in a rage, feeling indignant and self-righteous.*

You were aware of the event and the emotion, and probably felt you were entirely justified in feeling the way you did. In fact, when you asked yourself the burning question, 'Why do I feel this way?' you may well have felt it was a stupid question because it was obvious why you felt like that – look what he had done! You were probably quite unaware of the middle step – the self-talk. Perhaps after a few days you got tired of feeling so angry and found that you had better things to worry about.

If you had listened to your self-talk, however, you might have heard something like this:

'That was disgusting. Imagine anyone doing that to a friend! Bob has really hurt me. Friends don't behave that way. He's obviously no real friend. What a hypocrite! He's so selfish and thinks only of himself. He is totally untrustworthy – how dare he treat me like that!'

No wonder the anger grows and grows until it becomes excessive!

Now you may be aware of the little voice running in your head, feeding all these thoughts and emotions.

Sometimes it takes a little practice to identify the little voice, and to become aware of it. And of course, sometimes the thoughts that lead to your evaluation of the situation are so **habitual** that you are quite unaware that they are happening at all. This is what prejudice really is – decisions that have been made in advance and which are never **examined and tested** for their appropriateness or truth.

Once you have identified what the self-talk is, you will need to discover whether or not it is rational, and challenge it if it is not. So the process now looks like this:

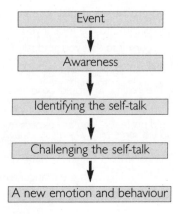

Let's go back to the example of your friend Bob, whose nasty behaviour upset you so much, and your reaction to his behaviour. How can you challenge your irrational reaction? We could take each thought and challenge it for rationality:

THOUGHT	CHALLENGE
Friends should not behave like that.	Why not? Who says friends should always behave in the way I think they should?
He's obviously not a real friend or he wouldn't have done that.	He has done something I don't like but does that mean he is not a real friend? He has done many other kind things for me.
What a hypocrite!	Does one nasty act make him a hypocrite? I don't like what he has done, but does that mean I can write off his sincerity like this?
Imagine doing that to a friend!	Maybe he's not perfect. Does being not perfect mean that he can't be a friend to anyone?

We could go on. By the end of the exercise, you will be feeling a lot calmer. You may well still be angry, but the anger will be manageable and probably more in proportion to what has happened. The underlying belief was, 'My friends must not do things like this to me' – overtones of the demanding Parent! You can apply this in the same way to situations in business and at home as well.

A more rational belief in the situation with Bob would have been, '*I would prefer it if my friends did not do things like that*'. It may sound as if changing 'must' to 'prefer' is only a play on words, but it is much more than that. It is changing your attitude. When you say, 'friends should/must …' you are in effect saying, 'I do not like reality: it should be different.' You may as well stamp your feet and jump up and down like a child in a tantrum!

When you say, 'I would prefer …' you are expressing a preference, rather than a need. You are not demanding that things be different, but accepting reality as it is. The emotional impact on *you* is quite different.

When you find yourself battling with great anger, resentment or anxiety at work, go through the same steps and examine all the assumptions in your

self-talk. You may well find that there are some quite irrational ones and then be able to change them. At the very least you will feel calmer. At best, you will be able to get back to productive work, and perhaps you may even be able to cooperate well with whoever has upset you, and learn to cope with their way of doing things.

Some irrational beliefs are more deep-seated than others and the more strongly we hold a belief the more difficult it is to change it. In the situation with Bob you may have had a deeply held belief about the way friends 'should be'. Because of this belief, it could be quite difficult to change your feelings for any length of time.

Talking about your feelings

You might be able to reduce your anger to a manageable level, but find it difficult to sustain. In quite a short time you may be back ranting and raving to yourself about the unfairness of the situation and the way things should be. You may therefore need to go through the process of challenging your self-talk **a number of times** before you are sufficiently calm to be able to talk to your friend about it.

Eventually you will succeed in reducing your anger to a manageable level and dealing with the situation constructively. You will then be able to tell your friend how you felt without blaming him – and **open up communication** in such a way that he will be able to tell you his perception of what happened. In this way, you may discover an aspect of the event that had escaped your notice, and the whole situation may be resolved.

If, on the other hand, you speak to him while you are still really angry, you are likely to have a confrontation, blaming him for your feelings and being aggressive. This may damage your relationship. Your relationship may also be damaged if you use the irrational thinking approach, deciding to say nothing about your feelings and withdrawing emotionally because of your anger. This will, unfortunately, not rid you of your anger. Your resentment will probably surface in a passive-aggressive manner.

This **constant checking** for the basis of your extreme feelings, and questioning whether that basis is rational and useful, will in time help you to become more aware of other people and their different feelings, needs and situations. This leads to a far more accommodating attitude, one that will make you feel much calmer and a great deal happier. You will find yourself getting upset less frequently, and this in turn will help you to feel better about yourself. In this way you are setting up a happy cycle of positive reinforcement in your interactions with others.

ADDICTION OR PREFERENCE?

In his book *A Conscious Person's Guide to Relationships*, Ken Keyes claims that if we get very, very upset about anything, it may indicate that we may have an addiction to it. People get addicted not only to alcohol, cigarettes or drugs, but also to abstract attributes such as punctuality, reliability, honesty, tidiness and perfection, to name a few. The problem with addictions is that they make the addict very uncomfortable if they are not satisfied. Just as the nicotine addict may become very twitchy if he cannot have a cigarette, you may become extremely agitated if your addiction to punctuality is not satisfied.

Ken Keyes claims that if you can change your addiction to a preference you will spend a lot less time being upset. Think for a moment what a preference is and why it is far more comfortable to live with than an addiction. You may have a preference for brown bread and not be so keen on white bread. But you are not addicted to brown bread. You do not have to have it. You will not crave it or be enraged if you do not get it. You can live quite comfortably with your preferences – they do not cause emotional discomfort if not satisfied.

For instance, let's assume you have an addiction to punctuality in social situations. When you make arrangements with a friend for a particular time and he is late, you will be furious. You may try various ways of dealing with your anger – pretending to yourself that you are not angry by rationalising away the feeling; knowing that you are angry but not expressing it directly; demanding that he be on time 'or else ...', making passive-aggressive digs about his tardiness. None of these will really help you.

If you could change your addiction to a preference, you could assertively ask him to be punctual next time.

You may have success with some people, but life being the way it is and people being the way they are, there will be times when people are not punctual. If you are addicted to punctuality, your evening or mood may be ruined at any time. When you start listening to yourself, you may discover that you are saying some of the things in the first column below. Challenge your thoughts as suggested in the second column:

THOUGHT	CHALLENGE
He should be on time.	Why should he? Who says this should be so? Is being late a crime? When history is written, will this be of any importance? Why am I upset about a few minutes?
He should be more reliable.	Why should he be reliable? Is being late in fact a sign of unreliability? He may be very reliable and he will always be there for me, but he may be quite easy-going about being on time.
Obviously, I'm not impor-tant to him – he doesn't care about me.	What makes me think that he is treating me any differently from anyone else for whom he cares? He may express his affection for me in a hundred other ways, but still be unable to keep his appointments punctually.

If you stop blaming your friend and take some of the responsibility yourself for your bad feelings about the incident, perhaps you will be able to do something about it.

We cannot usually change other people's behaviour, but *we can have control over whether or not it makes us deeply miserable.*

CHAPTER 5

Big Truths, Little Truths

*A true knowledge of ourselves
is knowledge of our power.*
MARK RUTHERFORD

Once we have come to grips with the power of the words we use in our minds – our self-talk – we can take the concept a little further. Just as the words we use and the thoughts we think can make us happy, angry, sad or frustrated, so they can have a very significant effect on all parts of our lives.

OTHER PEOPLE'S IDEAS

If you turn back to Chapter 3, you will find the exercise you did on 'I remember being told …' (see page 54). Have a look at what you wrote there. Then try to remember more of those voices from your childhood, as well as from more recent times. Try to remember voices that gave you messages about yourself – what you are and how people respond to you.

Some of these messages are wonderful, for example: 'You're gorgeous!' or 'You're so clever!' or 'I think you're fantastic!' Think of all the best things people have said to you over the years and write down as many as you can remember. Don't forget to quote the people who have been in love with you – they say the best ones!

THE BEST THINGS PEOPLE HAVE SAID TO ME ARE:

_____

_____

_____

_____

_____

Now try to remember some of the negative things people said, for example: 'You're so clumsy' or 'Why can't you do anything right?' or 'You'll be late for your own funeral one day.' They may be very hurtful indeed, like, 'I don't know why I ever had you!' or 'It's all your fault. If it wasn't for you I could have …'. Remembering these voices from the past may not be a pleasant experience, and for some of us, our early years are best not remembered at all. If that is the case, it may be better to think of some of the things your teachers said to you. They often seem not to realise how much they can hurt and disappoint us.

WRITE DOWN SOME OF THESE NEGATIVE MESSAGES:

_____

_____

_____

_____

_____

Did you remember anything like, 'Who asked you your opinion anyway?' or 'How can you ask such a thing?' or something like that wonderful line from *District Six, the Musical,* 'If I want your opinion, I'll give it to you!'

All these messages are still there in your mind, and they have a powerful bearing on the way you see yourself, whether you want them to or not.

PENDULUM POWER

Try this exercise. Tie a key or something slightly heavy to a piece of string. If you don't have string, use a ribbon, or a shoelace, or even take off your pendant and use that. We want a pendulum. Hold your hand very still so that the pendulum hangs still. While consciously holding your hand steady, imagine that the pendulum is swinging from left to right. Create a picture of it moving. It will begin to swing. The more clearly you see the picture, the more the pendulum will swing. Then change the picture in your mind. Create a picture of the pendulum swinging in a circle. It will change direction and start going round and round.

 Is this magic? Not at all. It simply demonstrates the power of pictures on the subconscious mind. While you are using your conscious mind to tell your hand to hold still, the picture you are seeing is informing your subconscious mind. It sees the picture and asks, 'Is that what you want? Not a problem!' and organises tiny muscular movements that cause the pendulum to swing to match the picture.

We call this process of informing the subconscious in pictures *visualising*. What is interesting is that the subconscious mind doesn't work in words at all. It deals only in pictures, and it receives every picture as an **instruction**. Add to that the information that visualisation is the main driving force of the body, and you can imagine the **power** you possess in the pictures of your mind! So it should be easy to understand why it is so important to look at the pictures we have of ourselves, and where they come from, so that we can change them if we wish to.

In a very real way, *the picture you have of yourself is what you will become*.

CHOOSING OUR TRUTHS

We have looked at how we **inherit ideas and values** from our early years. We have examined the way we develop **filters for interpreting life** at the present moment. We have considered the effect of positive and negative **messages** on the way we live and relate to people.

Now we are going to have a look at *what we can do to take control of all this thinking and these pictures.*

Imagine that your mind is like a picture gallery, hung with pictures of various sizes, up and down the walls. There are some wide, light rooms; there are some darker, more hidden rooms; there are some rooms you never even visit, where pictures are stacked against the walls in the dark.

These pictures reflect your idea of yourself, your memories and your dreams. Your daydreams are here, as well as your fears. When you wander through the gallery looking at them, some of these pictures show brief moments of your early life, frozen in time. Others are more recent, and are in strong colour.

They turn into videos when you stop to watch. Some of them are fun, but many are not. Some are embarrassing, or painful, or disappointing.

When someone asks you to describe yourself, you scan the walls and select a label or two from the largest, most brightly lit groups of pictures. These are your big truths, the attributes that you feel sum you up best, what you imagine the world sees of you.

But there are also some little truths in other pictures. Some may be very tiny, having only been true of you once or twice in your life. But they are still there, and they are still true.

You are the custodian of this gallery. You may decide what hangs on your walls, whether the general mood is positive and cheerful, or whether there is a feeling of failure and despair. You may also decide where to hang the various pictures, which ones will have spotlights on them, which will be big and which small. You may relegate pictures to the dark back-rooms, and you may bring out dusty old prints and have them restored into works of art.

Changing our truths

If you find that your big truths, the ones you spend the most time with, the pictures you generally have of yourself (and the ones you send to others), are not the most helpful, then you can choose to move the pictures in your gallery around. You can turn some little pictures into big ones, while you relegate the less helpful ones to a smaller, darker place.

> *When I first met Sandy, she was shy, unsure of herself and having difficulty forming and maintaining good relationships. Over the weeks of our sessions together, I discovered that she had had a sad childhood, with many disappointments and betrayals by those she loved and trusted most. Her 'big truths' about herself were that she was pretty worthless, that she had no right to expect much from life, that she would never amount to anything. The pictures hanging in her gallery depicted her failures in earning love, the many times she was unsuccessful in her attempts, and being let down and abandoned.*

She projected all these images of herself in subtle ways, and one could say that she unwittingly invited a negative response from people. Each time a relationship went wrong, each time another person left her or disappointed her, it reinforced her perception of the big truth about herself – that she was unlovable and a failure, and that she deserved nothing better than she was getting.

We began by looking at the little truths hiding away. Had she ever done anything she was really proud of? Yes, in primary school she had been the leader of a group which had done very well in a science competition. What 'truth' did that hold? We decided that it was that Sandy could organise well and get a team working together.

We took that truth and began to feed it. Had there been other occasions when she had demonstrated organising abilities? Other times when she had been involved in teams? We found some hidden away, cleaned them up and hung them under the spotlights in the first room of her mind. I encouraged her to say to herself as often as she could during the day, 'I'm a great organiser and a wonderful team playe.' And to stand in front of those pictures at night before going to sleep, watching and enjoying the scene of her success.

*There were other truths, too. We found that she had had a wonderful friendship with a girl in high school, until her friend's family had been transferred. We dusted off the happy pictures of being valued and sought out, and hung them in the front room too. Then we found an assortment of compliments and happy moments that had been stored facing the wall in case they weren't true enough, and brought them out. Each time I encouraged her to **spend time** viewing the scenes, reliving the moments and the feelings associated with them, finding the truth hidden in them and affirming that as true of herself. You see, even if something has been true only once, it is still a truth, albeit a tiny one.*

Gradually Sandy began to change. She smiled more. She walked differently. She laughed and sparkled. And people began to notice and enjoy her. Perhaps most importantly, she could even accept the times when people were not being nice to her. She had crossed over from needing to find her value in the opinions and actions of others, and had begun to take control of her own mental gallery and its values.

Simon Peter

One of the best examples of little truths turning into big truths may be found in the New Testament, in the story of Jesus and the fisherman, Simon. He is seen in the gospel narrative as a spontaneous, enthusiastic person, but unreliable. He meant well and was quick to make promises, but could as quickly move on to something else, and even get the next thing quite wrong. Up at Caesarea Philippi, Jesus said to him, 'You are Petros [rock]. On this rock I will build my Church and the gates of hell will not prevail against it.'

Perhaps the other disciples fell about laughing, thinking that Jesus had told one of his famous jokes. But Jesus was serious. He had spotted in Simon a *tiny* truth that nobody else had suspected. Simon received a new nickname – Peter – and gradually a new picture must have formed in his mind, for it grew into a big truth, and he changed. He became the head of the Church – wise, steady, faithful, unshakeable, like a rock. Today we call him St Peter, not St Simon.

What can the moral of this story do for you?

Choose your own big truths

Both Simon Peter and Sandy used the opportunity they were given to create a new set of pictures for themselves. Remember that your subconscious mind is the 'managing director' of your life, and that it receives every picture you spend time with as an instruction. You could take this opportunity to bring about a major difference in yourself by creating, and spending time with, a new set of pictures of your own choosing!

 Think of the little truths about yourself that you would like to turn into big truths. Perhaps you would like to become more confident. Have you ever been confident? Find the picture of that time or incident and move it into the bright lights of the front of your mind. Look at it often. Tell yourself as you walk along, 'I am a confident person and feel confident in all situations.' Paint a new picture of yourself being confident. What are you doing? What are you not doing? Include in your picture some other people looking admiringly at this confident person. Include some of your family or friends saying, 'My goodness, but you have changed. You have become so confident.' Make sure it is in glorious Technicolor and well lit. Spend time before you go to sleep every night examining the picture.

Within a few weeks people should be commenting on the difference, without your having to say anything at all.

Perhaps you would like to be peaceful and serene. Then ask yourself, 'Have I ever felt peaceful? Have I ever been serene, allowing the ups and downs of life and work to wash over me without becoming a victim to severe stress?' Catch those moments and hang the pictures of them in your gallery's front room. Imagine how you will be when you become more serene. Build up another picture of yourself, serene and peaceful, able to cope with anything and everything. You probably have a gentle smile on your face. Fill in the details. Visit it often, and within a short space of time serenity will begin operating in your life.

Remember that your subconscious mind operates only in pictures, and each time you feed it one of these pictures, it gets to work to make it true.

> **Be a good guardian of your gallery.**
> **Fill it with what is lovely, true, noble,**
> **loveable, and attractive, excellent,**
> **efficient and admirable. Then watch**
> **yourself as these little truths**
> **become your big truths.**

CHAPTER 6

It Doesn't Hurt to Ask

*To ask is no sin
and to be refused is no calamity.*
RUSSIAN PROVERB

There are requests and requests. Sometimes we need to ask a favour, and find it quite easy to do so. Other times we find it really difficult to ask someone to do us a favour. What is it that makes asking so hard? And why is it that so many of us find it so difficult to refuse the very requests we least want to say yes to?

Perhaps this is, in part, because the refusal of a request feels exactly like a **rejection of the person** asking. And none of us likes to be rejected. Most of us don't like to have others feel rejected either. So this becomes a complex problem.

MAKING REQUESTS

Many of us would much rather be on the giving than the receiving end, and asking favours can be extremely embarrassing for us. Perhaps it makes us feel weak or needy; or we feel ashamed or embarrassed if we cannot be self-sufficient. Perhaps we don't like people to come too close to us; allowing them to help us can sometimes bring about a certain intimacy in a relationship.

> *Rina had difficulty asking for anything. She often planned to ask others for help or for favours, but when it actually came to the point, she changed her mind. When I asked her why this was so, she replied, 'As soon as I see the person and want to ask her, I start remembering all the things she already does, and feel I shouldn't ask people to do things for me if I can do them myself. It seems lazy and that is horrible. It's not right to lean on others or let them wait on you hand and foot.'*

> *Rina felt it was better to be overworked or stretched to the limit, or to battle against huge odds trying to achieve the impossible, than to risk adding to someone else's workload. She seemed to have forgotten that asking does not necessarily guarantee a 'yes'. Could it be that she was afraid to ask for help because she knew that she was unable to refuse requests from others and, knowing the cost of saying yes against her better judgement, she was unwilling to put others in that situation?*

Let's look at some of the reasons why we are sometimes so unwilling to ask for help. Some of us are afraid our request will be refused, and then we will feel rejected. Some of us, like Rina, are afraid the person we ask will feel obliged to say yes, and what if he or she didn't really want to? Some of us are afraid people will think badly of us for asking. We sometimes say to ourselves, 'I don't have the right to ask …'

WRITE DOWN SOME THOUGHTS ON YOUR OWN RELUCTANCE TO ASK FAVOURS:

_____

_____

_____

_____

Playing games

Sometimes, and most of us would hate to admit this aloud, we don't want to express our needs or wants because of the game we are playing.

There are several kinds of games people play – you probably know them:

Read my mind …

'If I have to ask you for what I want, then you don't love me. If you did love me, you'd know what I want without my having to say, because you would be tuned in to me, or your intuition should tell you (or read my mind …)' (see page 39).

That is, of course, irrational, since mind-reading is not one of the skills people normally have, even when they love others.

The independence game

'I am strong. I am wise. People look up to me and I get things right. When I'm around, people feel better because I'm able to sort out everything. People depend on me – I am important. And I dare not be weak or I will lose that importance. So I cannot ask for help, or for advice, or for favours, unless I ask on behalf of someone else, of course.'

This is a game of independence. The truth of the matter, however, is that we have a right to ask, and the people we approach have the right to say yes or no as they see fit. In fact, being honest in our asking is a very great compliment to others. And we don't have the right to set others up for failure by making them play guessing games which they are sure to lose.

Sacrificial rituals

Our family used to specialise in a strange sort of sacrificial ritual. It went something like this:

> Dad: 'Who would like to go to the beach?' (remembering that he had a family and wishing to make amends for paying so little attention to them).

> We: 'Wonderful idea!' (thinking: In this wind? So late in the day? How awful! But poor Dad loves the beach and he is being so sweet. Let's not disappoint him!).

> Dad: 'Are you sure it's not too late or too windy?' (thinking: Maybe they won't really want to and I can be let off – it will probably be awful).

> We: 'No, its perfect!' (thinking: He's so sensitive – he is ready to forgo his pleasure in case our hairdo's are messed up. What a dear. We will go, whatever the cost).

So we go and it is awful and everyone hates it and sometimes we even end up grumpy and miserable. Why didn't anyone say no? Why didn't anyone speak out about their real feelings?

Have you ever gone to see the wrong film because you both thought the other wanted to see it, and both were being heroic by not saying what you really wanted? Both were sure they knew what the other was thinking, and both were wrong!

Honesty and trust

If I ask you for what I really want, it means I trust you with the knowledge of who I am and of my situation. And I treat you as an adult, with both the ability to make up your own mind and the facility to trust me with the real answer. What a pleasure. Then both of us know exactly where we stand and what each of us really feels.

We need to know that we can believe each other so that we can make realistic decisions. If you withhold the truth from me, I can't possibly get it right when I want to please you, can I? It's not usually helpful to tell lies about anything, even about how we feel, and certainly, it is arrogant to suppose that we know what is best for everyone (see page 30).

It is, after all, arrogant to suppose that we can read other people's minds. We thought we were decoding Dad so cleverly. He was guessing at what we thought and wanted. We also knew that all of us were prepared to be martyrs and so could not be relied on to tell the truth. Situations like this become incredibly complex. If I say that I don't want to go to the beach, someone is bound to think that I really do want to go and am just saying that to be heroic, in case the others don't want to go, and so we go in circles.

What a waste of effort, time, petrol and affection!

 Take a bit of time now to think about why you sometimes find it difficult to ask. There may be various reasons, relating to different people (who is it that you are trying to impress with your competence and self-sufficiency?). Perhaps you find asking easy. Examine this too.

Write down whether/when you find it easy or difficult to ask, and why:

_____

_____

_____

_____

_____

Be rational about refusal

Whatever you discover your main problem to be, start applying the tests of rational, logical thinking to it (see page 69). Are you confusing yourself with a lot of irrational untruths? Are you perhaps preventing others from doing things for you because of your own pride or fear?

Just as disagreeing with someone does not imply rejection, so refusing a request does not mean that you are rejecting the person. Just as people have the right to their own opinions, so they have the right to ask for whatever it is they want, and so do those being asked have the right to apply their own standards to evaluate the request.

Naturally there are moments that are more appropriate for making requests, and other moments that are less appropriate. Some requests will be appropriate in some societies and not at all in others, but you never-theless have the right to ask, although it helps to be aware of any possible sensitivities!

It is not rational to avoid making requests in case the other person feels cornered by it, or obliged to say yes. Nor is it rational to think that, because we have asked, the other person should agree to our request. We have the right to make up our own minds in line with our own value systems. Others have the same right.

We also have the right to resist manipulation by others, and we have the responsibility of not trying to manipulate them.

HOW TO ASK FOR WHAT YOU WANT

It seems to me that people are often unaware of what a certain choice of words or various tones of voice can do to a request. What left one per-son's mind as a quite pleasant, straightforward question may reach the other's mind as a demand or even an attack. So much depends on how it is done, and that is determined by the group of behaviours we are applying at the moment.

Let's look at some examples of formulating requests using the communi-cation model we developed in Chapter 2 (see page 28), and the possible effects they may have and the responses they may elicit.

Group 1: Aggressive controlling requests

Suppose you would like your partner to help you with the washing up. Think of one or two ways of expressing this if you were behaving according to Group 1. Use the aggressive controlling mind-set.

WRITE DOWN YOUR REQUESTS:

_____

_____

_____

_____

Some suggestions could be, 'Go and do the dishes. It's your turn!' or 'Get off your backside and do the washing up. It's not going to do itself!' or 'Time to do the washing up!' Can you see that in each case the speaker makes the decision for the other without reference to how he or she feels or what he or she wants? Whether it is meant kindly or not, whether the comment on the attitude of the other is a joke or not, the actual message is aggressive in its lack of empathic listening.

When someone makes a request in that way, how do you feel? Does it make you want to help? Does it make you feel rebellious? Naturally, it depends on who is asking and whether you feel they have the right to do it like that, but I suspect that whoever it is, you are likely to feel at least a twinge of resentment, anger or rebellion.

Group 2: Passive manipulating requests

Now have a go at Group 2 possibilities. You won't be direct here and actually say what you want. There may well be an element of hidden resentment, either against the one you are asking or even against life itself, or a kind of sarcastic dig, and it is likely that Darling will not be able to reply easily.

WRITE DOWN YOUR REQUESTS:

_____

_____

_____

_____

There are a vast number of possibilities, and here are some:
- 'There's no point bothering to ask *you* to do the washing up. If I want anything done around here, I have to do it myself.'
- 'Why hasn't anyone done the washing up?'
- 'I'm the only one who ever lifts a finger around this house.'

Or perhaps this conversation takes place:

> *(Very sweetly, but often **after** the washing up is finished) 'You know, if you really loved me that much you would have helped me with the washing up.' (Notice that it is in the past tense. Too late to jump up and help now.)*
>
> *'Just ask me when you want help – I don't mind at all', Darling replies.*
>
> *'If you really loved me I wouldn't have to ask. You'd notice without being told.'*

In each case there is manipulative behaviour, designed to induce a feeling of guilt or anxiety in the other person. In each case it seems that feelings of being a victim or martyr are being expressed. In each case, the other person would spoil the game if he leapt to his feet and actually did the washing up. Then you would have to say, 'Well, what's come over you?' or 'Got a sudden rush of blood to the head?' or something like that. Or, more commonly, 'Oh, don't bother. (Or 'Please don't put yourself out for me') I'll manage. You just relax and enjoy yourself' (while I slave away, obviously).

 How do you feel when someone else plays this game with you? Do you think it is effective? We may not like to admit it, but we all play this game some time or another, especially when we are feeling powerless. But I don't think it is a useful way of dealing with others, and as soon as you notice that you are doing it, ask yourself whether this is a relationship that you would like to develop, to improve, or to keep. If you care for and would like to keep this relationship, stop what you are doing and make a conscious effort to move into Group 4.

Group 3: Passive pleasing requests

How would you ask your partner to help you if your behaviour falls in the third group?

WRITE DOWN YOUR SUGGESTIONS:

_____

_____

_____

_____

Exactly how you ask in a Group 3 frame of mind, would depend on how far into the quadrant your behaviour falls. You may come up with something like the following:

> 'If you have a moment (or aren't too busy), would you mind giving me a hand with this washing up?' and if the other person sounded unenthusiastic, you would back off and say, 'Oh don't worry – it's not really a problem at all. I'm just being lazy.'

And if your partner did help, there would be a tremendous amount of thanking and appreciation afterwards!

If you moved further into the third quadrant, you would not easily come up with the request at all. There may be something like this:

> 'Darling?'
>
> 'Hmmm?'
>
> 'Oh never mind. It's not important.'
>
> 'What was it?'
>
> 'Nothing. I was just being silly', you say (sadly, because Darling didn't take the hint and think of offering).

This can be a bit tiresome, don't you think? Are you ever guilty of such half-hearted requests? How do you feel when you are on the receiving end? What does it say about you when you are the guilty party? Is that the message you want to get across?

Group 4: Free responsible requests

If you found those difficult to do, you will be pleased to know that the fourth quadrant request is much easier!

SEE HOW MANY VARIATIONS YOU CAN FIND AND WRITE THEM DOWN:

_____

_____

_____

_____

In the fourth group, your request would be brief and to the point: 'I'd really like it if you would give me a hand with the washing up.'

Then Darling may agree or not as he or she sees fit. There can be all kinds of negotiations arising out of the request. And everyone knows what it is about, and everyone can make an adult response to the situation. There will be no hard feelings, no guessing games, no manipulation, no damage to the relationship.

Direct, honest asking is a lovely thing

Now try it in the work context. How would you ask someone for some information you need very urgently? Which behaviour pattern is likely to be the most effective? Many people opt for those in Group 1 in the mistaken belief that a show of power impresses people and gets quick results. Usually what feels like power to you may look like bad manners or bad temper to others, and far more is usually gained by a direct, polite request.

Sometimes people feel that they need to be subtle and therefore resort to the manipulative, wheedling sweetness of a Group 2 request, starting with flattery and continuing with, 'I hope it's not too much to ask for …' in a sweet, insincere voice. I'm sure you recognise the sort of thing.

 Think of how you respond to the different styles of making requests and consider which makes you feel most cooperative, most inclined to agree.

Only those who are strong, those who are secure in their sense of their own value, those who are confident, are able to be pleasant and direct.

People respect those who say what they mean and who respect others as adults as well.

FORMULATING REQUESTS

In order to avoid manipulative behaviours which violate other people's right to decide for themselves, the requests we make should generally be:

- our own and not made on behalf of others, as the case would be in, 'Everyone thinks you should …' or 'Some people …' and so on;
- specific, with sufficient information for the other person to make a good evaluation;
- brief, honest and to the point, without embroidering or labouring the point, which will only cause confusion; and
- open to negotiation.

Emotional blackmail, threats, repeated pleading and begging do not have a place in responsible requests.

Take a moment to think of requests you would like to, or perhaps even need to, make to someone and that you have not yet been able to bring yourself to do for some reason or another. Maybe you need to ask for a raise in salary; maybe you would like to move into a different office, or a different division; maybe you want to apply for a study loan or a bursary for your child; maybe you want your husband to be more helpful around the house, or your teenage daughter not to use your make-up without asking. Use the guidelines above to formulate unmanipulative, clear requests. Then write them down and **be prepared to actually make them!**

I AM GOING TO MAKE THE FOLLOWING REQUESTS:

_____

_____

_____

_____

THE SOFT ANSWER – *YOU* CAN DECIDE

In the book of Proverbs in the Bible, the Preacher says, 'A soft answer turns away wrath.' Note that he does *not* say, 'A **yes** answer turns away wrath'.

Our responses to other people's requests are as complicated by all kinds of irrational and untrue thoughts as our feelings about asking.

Elize was a pushover for everyone's requests. It simply wasn't in her nature to refuse anyone who asked for a favour. She spent her days in her car, driving people to places, fetching shopping, dry-cleaning and groceries for others, at the same time looking after her grandchildren while their parents did whatever it was they wanted to, and drawing money to pay other people's debts.

She used to complain that her husband was very unsympathetic because he criticised her for all she did for others. He was disabled and many were the hours he spent in an unbearably hot car, parked in the sun on the side of the road, while Elize 'just quickly' gave someone a hand with their washing or whatever it was they were doing.

It seemed that she could not say no to the demands made on her by others, although she could most easily say no to his demands, because he was not 'other people' and, as part of herself, he should have had the same self-sacrificing attitude as she had.

> *The worst difficulties came when each of her four children made different demands on her, and she agreed to help others at the same time. She was always in a rush, could never be relied on for anything, was late for most things and spent her time in a haze of guilt and anxiety.*

For Elize, helping others was not a matter of joy but of assuaging guilt and being driven by an overdeveloped sense of obligation. 'I should' and 'I ought to' were her main motivation, rather than 'I could' or 'I'd like to'.

> *At the other extreme was James, who as a matter of principle avoided doing anything anyone asked of him. He was so afraid that others would take advantage of him that he said no to requests without ever first finding out what his real, deep feeling was. And because his responses were motivated by fear, his refusals tended to be loud, defensive and unfriendly. After his parents died, his only sister gave up trying to be friends with him, and gradually he became lonelier and lonelier, alienated from other people by his fear of being used.*

She couldn't say no, and he couldn't say yes. Both of these people were totally out of touch with their feelings and both were driven by fear – the one of being thought of as unkind, and the other of being taken advantage of. Both were deeply unhappy and unfulfilled.

Make your own decision

When you get down to it, there are really only three things you can do with a request.

- You can say yes to it;
- You can say no to it; or
- You can put off the answer until there is more information to hand, or until you have conferred with the other interested parties, or until you have had sufficient time to think about it.

Say what you mean

If you decide that you will say yes, then begin your reply with 'Yes …' so that there is no confusion. By the same token, if you are going to refuse the request, let the 'No …' feature early in the first sentence. That means that the other person is in no doubt as to what you are really saying.

Suppose you feel sad about refusing a request and you start with your feelings. You could cause this to happen:

> *'Sally, I really am so happy that you asked me to do this for you. You know how much I care about you and Bob and nothing would make me happier than to be able to do what you ask ...'*
>
> *At this point you are about to continue, '... but unfortunately ...'. However, Sally gets in first and throws her arms around you, kissing and hugging you in gratitude.*

Now try to get out of that! Not only will she be disappointed, but you and she will both be embarrassed and feel most awkward. It would have been far better if you had started with the 'No ...' and then gone on, after the disappointment had worn off, to tell her how you feel.

She may not be able to hear and take in your loving message right then if the disappointment is very great, and it could be that there will be another, better time for getting that particular message across.

It is very important that you allow people to understand right away what the reply is going to be. Have you ever been in the position where someone is beating about the bush and you are in agony waiting to find out what their intentions are? They do it all the time when announcing the results of competitions, don't they?

A shorter and more common form of the 'Sally ...' answer is the 'I'd love to, but unfortunately ...'. Somehow the 'but' tends to cancel out a lot of the 'I'd love to' message. A straight 'no' has so much impact that the chances are the other person will actually listen to what follows!

 It is worth doing a bit of listening and noting to come to grips with this aspect of effective communication. When you hear people asking, accepting and refusing, watch to see what happens. Try to identify what is happening and what the effects of the different kinds of reply are.

NOTE SOME OF YOUR OBSERVATIONS HERE:

_____

_____

_____

_____

Take note particularly of how **you** feel when others respond to a request you make.

Which kind of response do you really prefer?

_____

_____

_____

_____

It is certainly true that it is easier to deal with a definite answer, whether it is the one we wanted or not, than to deal with an uncertainty. Even the worst disappointments can be handled once they have happened, but when we consider the possibility of disappointment, we feel as if we will never cope. It is kinder and more pleasant all round to speak out with the truth, and to give the real answer first time.

Steps in dealing with requests

The first thing to do is to *make sure that you have understood the request.* Some requests are quite obvious and plain. Some are not. If I were to ask my friend if I could borrow her husband, she may well be quite shocked. Unless she discovered that I wanted help turning the temperature down on my geyser!

To make certain that you have understood, either ask for more information, or paraphrase the request back.

'Please may I borrow your husband?'

'You'd like to borrow my husband. Is there something special you'd like him to do for you?'

'Yes, I'd like him to help me by climbing into the ceiling and turning down the temperature of my geyser.'

'He probably won't mind, but perhaps you should ask him!'

When someone is asking you a favour that might turn out to be bigger than it first appears, like looking after her children while she and her husband go out, it would be well to establish all the details before making your decision.

You may also want to take the second step, which is to ask for time to think it through. Away from the situation and the possible pressure, things may look much clearer.

You may also wish to *consult* anyone else who would be involved. You may need to check with your spouse or children. You may need to mention it to others whose plans would be affected. Then decide and reply.

Don't get trapped by fears and anxieties
So far, it has probably not been too difficult. Bur when it comes to the reply itself, our worst fears and anxieties come into play.

What if the other person is upset? What if he or she no longer likes me? What if my refusal ruins all their plans? What if I say no now and then when I want a favour, they refuse me? What if I am wrong to say no and I should be saying yes?

These are all very real anxieties and ones that can trap us into an awful lot of unnecessary distress. Some of us were brought up to believe that we are only placed on this earth for the benefit of others, and that our wishes, needs and desires are not important. In fact, some of us are taught that if our needs or desires are in conflict with anything asked for by another, we should, in every case, back down and serve the other. This may sound noble, but it is not a useful way to live. For one thing, we lay ourselves open to burn-out in our efforts to please everyone, and for another, we become very bad at caring for and maintaining our own physical and mental health. We may then become a serious burden on friends, family or society at large. A balanced approach is a far better investment in the future.

No-one is indispensable
How arrogant we sometimes are in our sense of our own importance! It seems that we reason, 'If I say no to this person, he or she will fall to pieces,' or 'If I say no, he or she will not cope, and there will be no-one else to help. I am the only one who can really do this well …'

The need to be indispensable plays on the proud and self-seeking aspects of our nature. It is good to feel wanted, and is very often wonderful to feel that you are the one whom everyone turns to in times of need. It is more difficult and more humble to say no and allow others to be adult and find their own solution. This is even more difficult when the other person is your son or your daughter. But you need to allow them the growth experience of coping them-selves with the problems of their lives, and maybe even making mistakes. It is so much easier to rescue them and to provide solutions, than to allow them to make their own mistakes and spend their own sleepless nights.

We do our children a great disfavour when we feed our own parental needs by 'being there for them' every time they want help. In the long run we actually **disempower** them. The same can be said for all those people who have been socialised into a 'child' dependent role and who now have the opportunity to be adult in society and take responsibility for themselves.

Changing your reply habits

The best thing of all is to take the risk of radical change in your reply habits. When you are able to change 'I can't' into 'I won't' you may well have crossed the line from dishonesty to real honesty and at the same time made your life a little less complicated. Consider this scenario:

> *Joe asks me out to dinner. I don't really like him and have no wish to get involved with him. I don't want to hurt his feelings, so I reply, 'I'd love to, but I'm afraid I can't. I've got to spend the evening with my parents.'*
>
> *He then suggests the next evening and I have to have another excuse. He suggests the weekend, and I have to think up something else. So it could go on, with poor Joe beginning to suspect that he has halitosis, or that there is something awful wrong with him that I can't bear to tell him about.*
>
> *He says, 'I think I'm making a fool of myself. You don't want to go out with me, do you?'*
>
> *I'm so embarrassed that I lie, 'Of course I do. It's just that it is a little difficult at the moment …'*

We both know that I am lying. He now has to lie awake at night worrying about what it is that is so awful that it can't be said, and whether everyone else knows and thinks badly of him.

Had I said in the beginning, 'No, Joe, I'd prefer us just to go on meeting casually here,' he could have asked why, and I could have said that I felt we had very little in common. That is no judgement on him, merely a statement of my perception of difference, and it would be far less hurtful to his self-image. He could even, if he wished, decide to try again later when we have got to know each other better.

Either way, I have treated him like an adult, paid him the compliment of an honest reply, and I have not exposed him to uncertainty which, as we have seen, is difficult to handle. Besides, I have also not led myself into a pattern of lies and dishonesty. After all, all he has done is ask me out once!

I could even tell him what I like about him and he might enjoy that, but I would comfortably stick with my decision about dinner: 'I'd rather not, thank you.'

Watchpoints

When you reply to requests, beware of the following:

The 'compassion trap'

This makes you feel that if you don't do what is asked, the other person will be in a dreadful situation and it will be your fault. We get a great deal of this today, especially with people who feel the world owes them something.

Some people hook into your natural compassion and try to build up a level of anxiety and guilt that will manipulate you into doing what they ask against your better judgement.

We often, quite correctly, feel sorry for people, and to have compassion is good. But to be trapped by people who wish to trade on our better nature, and who know which 'buttons' to press to make us feel bad, is certainly not good.

The need to build up 'credits'

Here people say something along the lines of, 'Well, then don't expect me to do anything for you,' as if there were some ledger book in which we could build up or use credit with others. There isn't.

There is nothing that records that you owe me three favours, or that I owe you a good turn.

The 'unspoken threat' trap

Here you get the uncomfortable feeling that you had better do what is being asked, or else … Don't allow yourself to be manipulated by such an attitude.

Know what is asked

Make sure that you completely understand the request and what it involves and decide what is **appropriate** in that situation. Understand that everything has its price, for example doing something you would rather not do, and also sometimes refusing to do something you would rather not do.

It is your decision and, while *you can choose your action, you cannot choose the consequences!*

> No matter how excellently a man's soul may be
> inclined to the performance of a good action,
> in ninety cases out of a hundred he is driven away
> by dread of the consequences.
> WILLIAM J LOCKE

'I can't' versus 'I won't'

There is no need to justify your decision to refuse unless you want to. The fact that you have made up your own mind is sufficient, and very often the less you say, the more seriously you will be taken. People will often demand a reason for your refusal, but that still does not imply an obligation on your part to supply your reason. Your thought processes, your evaluation and your preferences are your own business.

Note, however, that often in close relationships a lot more explanation and negotiation are called for. It is hurtful and alienating to refuse to discuss decisions with your nearest and dearest and will do little to improve your relationship and trust. Be aware though, that manipulation is all too frequently encountered here too and needs to be dealt with in much the same way as with someone who is not close to you.

 It is more definite, more powerful and more final to say, 'I prefer not to' or 'I don't want to' or 'I have decided against it' than to try to find excuses for why 'I can't'.

If you can't, **there has to be a reason,** and as soon as we get into reasons or excuses, it is an invitation to others to argue the point, or to solve the 'difficulties'. Words that indicate a *decision* that you have made (I won't), rather than a *situation* that prevents you (I can't) tend to end the discussion.

In fact, you are not obliged to explain your decision to the person who has made the request, so it needn't be 'I can't'. It will often be unwise to explain, especially if the person is trying to manipulate you and twist your arm. The more you say, the more they are able to argue the point. Again, you can take refuge in, 'No, I won't: I have weighed up the factors and come to my decision.'

The more the other person tries to change your mind, the less friendly your reply may become, but that is not necessarily a bad thing. You have to resist being made to do things against your better judgement. If we allow others to manipulate us we are not taking responsibility for our own actions, and we are behaving below the line in our model.

There is a technique called 'Broken Record' which you can use when someone is persistent. It consists of doing just what you would expect from the name. You go on repeating the same thing over and over until the other person gives up.

Say your daughter wants to borrow your car and will not accept no for an answer. You simply answer everything she says with the same refusal, whether she asks a question or makes a statement. Don't be drawn into answering any questions. Just stick with your decision. The conversation could go something like this:

> 'Mom, please can I borrow your car tonight?'
>
> 'No. I prefer not to lend my car to anyone.'
>
> 'Not even me?'
>
> 'Not anyone.'
>
> 'But why not?'
>
> 'I prefer not to.'
>
> 'But I won't hurt it. I'll be really careful and I'll put in petrol.'
>
> 'I prefer not to lend my car to anyone.'
>
> 'Don't you trust my driving, hey Mom?'
>
> 'I prefer not to lend my car to anyone.' … and so on.

You can see that after a while the conversation is going to become very boring indeed and your daughter must eventually get the message that the car is simply not available, with no reasons that can be argued with. You are dealing with your own right to decide on the basis of your feelings and preference. You win.

 Think of a recent situation recently when someone has managed to get you to change your mind and agree to something you didn't want to agree to. How did you say no to begin with? What did he or she do that successfully made you change your mind? How did you feel? Could you have handled it differently?

Write all of this down:

_____

_____

_____

_____

_____

Blaming it on others

An interesting variation of the 'I can't' versus 'I won't' situation is what arises when we bring up our children.

We may find that we use all kinds of crutches to gain credibility in our decision-making. We may say, 'Good children don't do that,' as if there were some universal ruling on the behaviour of 'good children' that we could take out of the library and swot up. Then we include the opinions of other people as if we knew what they were thinking ('People will think you are a horrible child').

It would be far more honest, and would lead to far less anxiety and guilt in later life on the part of our children, if we as parents let it be known that, 'I don't want you to do that' and 'I don't like it when you …' and 'I'd prefer it if you would …' instead of appealing to these external 'laws'.

The huge load of suspected general censure would fall away like magic from the shoulders of children, teenagers and adults alike.

 Go back to some of the messages you wrote down when you did the exercise of remembering influences from your childhood in Chapter 3 (see page 54). So many of the really inhibiting and damaging (and irrational) messages involved other people and their opinions, didn't they? If our parents had come out honestly and taken responsibility themselves for what they taught us, we might very well be having a much easier time evaluating and changing our behaviours now. Don't repeat their mistakes with your own children.

CHAPTER 7

A Matter of Opinion

*Our lives begin to end
the day we become silent
about things that matter.*
MARTIN LUTHER KING

Everyone is entitled to an opinion. We may make up our own minds, and we have the right to our opinions, whether they differ from those of others or not. When we were young many of our opinions were formed for us, and often we had the feeling that it was not okay to express what we really thought in case we exposed ourselves to more correction, sometimes ridicule, and even punishment. When our opinions were not what they were 'supposed to be', we felt anxious, ignorant and guilty.

Many of us still have the uncomfortable feeling that our own opinions are not as good or as valuable as the opinions of others, and we spend a lot of our time feeling those same sad emotions of childhood — guilt, anxiety and ignorance.

> The scars left from the child's defeat in the
> fight against irrational authority are to be found
> at the bottom of every neurosis.
> ERICH FROMM

EVERYONE HAS THE RIGHT TO AN OPINION

The truth is that we are entitled to be right or wrong as we wish. There is no law anywhere that says I have to be right, or that I may not make mistakes. If I hold an opinion, I may express it if I wish. You don't have to agree with me, and if you don't, that creates no value judgement on either you or me. Neither of us has the right to name, blame or shame the other for that opinion. What we **can** do is explore how that opinion relates to the facts as they are perceived, and discuss it from there.

CHOOSING SILENCE

There are many unfortunate people who feel unsafe about expressing their opinions. They sit in meetings and think valuable and interesting thoughts, and nobody knows that, because they never tell them. If you ask them why they don't share some of their thoughts, they may tell you something like this:

'I don't have anything worthwhile to say – I'm sure the others have already thought of my ideas.' Or, 'No, I can't speak up – everyone else knows so much more than I do! They'll think I'm stupid.'

Both of these hint at some very common and fundamental errors in thinking that people have about expressing opinions. One is that an opinion has to be new, deep, different or important before it can be expressed. Another is that you have to be an expert on the subject before you have the right to speak. Yet another is that other people have the right to reject or laugh at the person who comes up with something that has already been considered, or which may be factually incorrect.

There are also those who, for some reason or another, are stuck in a Group 2 mode and decide to keep their opinions to themselves because they do not wish to share them with others.

They are not afraid their opinions are unacceptable: they are too angry or resentful to allow others the benefit of their contribution. They choose to remain silent, and for them, as for the others, the choice is likely not to be a conscious one. They probably also have no idea why they act this way. All they know is that they don't want to participate in meetings, or that they couldn't be bothered.

Let's look at the reasons why people choose silence, one at a time.

An opinion has to be new or different

An opinion is simply the way you think, or the way you perceive reality. And the way you perceive things may feel very normal and ordinary to you, but be quite a revelation to someone else. It may not seem new and exciting to you at all, but still be very worthwhile in a conversation or discussion.

It is not necessary to be an intellectual giant to have opinions worth expressing. Holding them is enough reason to share them.

Opinions may only be expressed by experts

If this were true, very little would ever be discovered – it's often the uninformed opinions of people who have not gone into depth on a subject that stimulate the thoughts of the real experts in new, exciting directions. Why did Edison fly kites in the lightning? Possibly because someone who knew nothing about physics then, and who didn't know that it was quite impossible, said it would be nice to catch the brightness of lightning and hang it inside the room. We'll never know. But the principle is there. If you have an opinion that isn't informed, speak out – you may trigger a new line of thought in an expert's mind!

And you will be surprised how often you come up with something that is perfectly obvious to you and that nobody else has ever thought of!

People might mock me if I am wrong

This is to misunderstand completely the nature of an opinion. If I say 'I think …' or 'It seems to me …' or 'What about …', then I am expressing my idea on something. I am not pretending to tell the facts, nor am I trying to tell others what they should think. I am really opening negotiations, throwing out an idea which may or may not be useful in the discussion.

There is a vast difference between 'It's freezing today' and 'I think it's freezing today.' Can you see it? The first states a fact. Now if the temperature is actually in the high twenties at the time, it may be a rather strange thing to say, because a verifiable fact has been wrongly stated. The second statement, however, is always true and acceptable. At the worst, the person may be ill, but not strange or wrong. That person's opinion is exactly that – what that person perceives – and each one of us is entitled to express what we perceive. Remember that no-one has to agree with you if they don't wish to, but their disagreement is not a rejection of you – it's merely a different view being expressed.

Unfortunately not everyone is logical, and there may well be people who do laugh at others who express different opinions. It does happen. Comfort yourself with the knowledge that you are correct and entitled to your opinions, and that they are the ones who are out of line.

Firstly, I don't believe that there is ever any value in laughing at or rejecting other human beings, especially for something they have said. And secondly, your opinion expresses how you view and understand something. That is valid, and if it can be disproved it simply shows that you had misread the facts, or been misled by them, or had a different way of interpreting them. A lot of what is 'wrong' now, in terms of science or even human relations, may well be 'right' in a few years' time! (Think of the butter versus margarine debate: first butter was bad for you, now it is good for you!)

Anyway, you are always free to change your mind and see something differently, if you want to, but you are the owner of your thoughts and your perceptions, and you are entitled to voice your opinion whenever it is appropriate to the situation.

DIFFERENCES OF OPINION

What about opinions of liking and disliking? What if you want to tell people that you don't like what they are doing or saying? Or if the people you are with all like something and you think it is horrible? Can you then still say what is on your mind? What does this say about you?

In fact, it says nothing other than that you hold a different view from the others. Of course you can say what is on your mind – everyone is entitled to an opinion, and is responsible for that opinion.

But it can sometimes happen that the group doesn't appreciate a different opinion, and they may shut you out, or scoff at you. Sometimes the person you are speaking to may try to make you feel stupid or wrong to have said what you did. What does this say about you, or the other person? Does this make them right? It says nothing about you at all, but it does say something sad about the others. It says that they are not able to cope with differences of opinion, and that is impoverishing.

> In all matters of opinion
> our adversaries are insane.
> MARK TWAIN

Think about what makes for richness in taste, in texture, in experience, in life. Differences! Perhaps the time has come for us in South Africa to start treasuring, rather than fearing, our differences. And such liberation will begin with our freedom to express differences of opinion and viewpoint. It will be easier to do this at certain times and in certain situations than in others.

Be prepared to pay the price

It cannot be said too often that *freedom is being able to choose which price you wish to pay*. For there is a price on everything in life. There is a price on speaking up and there is a price on remaining silent. There is a price on being

honest and there is a price on being dishonest. Generally the price on being dishonest is far greater than on being honest, certainly in the long term, and that is why we say that 'Honesty is the best policy' – it pays to be honest!

But we need to understand the cost of whatever it is that we want to do. If I decide that I can't take the risk of having people laugh at me, then it could be argued that I am right in deciding to keep quiet.

If, on the other hand, I am frustrated because people never take my views into consideration, then maybe the cost of possibly being laughed at is not too high to pay.

> **You are free to choose any action you wish, but you are not free to choose the consequences.**

CHOOSE WITH RESPONSIBILITY

You are the only one who can decide whether you will choose silence or expressing your opinion. Only you can decide what price you are prepared to pay, and it may vary from one day to another.

You are not wrong, whatever you decide, provided that you accept the responsibility for the decision and do not afterwards blame everyone else for the price **you** have chosen to pay.

Why is it difficult to express your opinion?

Bearing all that in mind, let's consider some of the things that sometimes make it difficult for you specifically to feel confident about expressing opinions. If you don't have difficulty with this, then move on to the next section.

WHAT DO OTHERS DO THAT MAKES ME UNWILLING OR RELUCTANT TO SPEAK UP?

_____

_____

_____

_____

WHAT ASPECTS OF MYSELF CONTRIBUTE TO THIS — BELIEFS, HABITS, MESSAGES RECORDED IN MY PARENT EGO STATE? (see Chapter 3, page 54)

_____

_____

_____

_____

COMMUNICATION AND FREEDOM OF EXPRESSION

Real communication is impossible when people are not free to take the risk of stating their opinions and disclosing their thoughts. Part of our responsibility for our own wellbeing is to **make ourselves known** as we are, so that people are able to deal with us in the way we wish them to. Part of our responsibility is also **not to violate the right of other people to express their opinions and make their opinions known.**

Have another look at the model of communication (see page 28). In Groups 2 and 3, part of the main problem is that when people behave like that, they don't say what is on their mind. That makes it impossible for others to know how to respond to them. It prevents any real communication, and any development of good relationships from taking place. When people behave in this way they are trapped behind the Silence Barrier, and those around them are also affected by it.

Constructive, assertive communication improves the quality of relationships by making them more real. We deal with each other as we really are, and not as we expect others to want us to be. But this does not mean that there will be no conflict. People are not always the way we want them to be, and when we discover the areas of difficulty, we have to work hard at our relationships. There is a price on everything and although some people are less able to deal with differences than others, the price of hard work and honesty is usually a small one to pay for the rewards we receive.

When we all reach the point where we **value** our differences rather than **fear** them, both we and our country will be in a much better position to build good relationships. It is incredibly empowering to be able to express your opinion as it is, without being afraid of being wrong, or upsetting people, or feeling foolish – or even going to prison! Unfortunately, many of us have been brought up not to speak out, especially if what we think is different from the family's opinions, the opinions of older people or those of the group. We need to realise that we can change that and break the barrier of silence that brings so much confusion.

COMPLIMENTARY OPINIONS

The opinion we wish to express may be positive and relate to others and their behaviour. Giving and receiving compliments is generally rather nice, but for some reason many people find it difficult.

Paying compliments

We'll start with paying compliments. Are you nervous of speaking out in case the other person takes it amiss? It is not rational to suppose that all people feel uncomfortable when we compliment them, nor that they suspect us of ulterior motives! It is worthwhile paying compliments when they are warranted, and they can in fact go a long way to helping good relationships develop.

Be **honest** in your compliments, and be brief, and specific. Avoid overdoing it (and thereby taking away all their value), avoid sarcasm and above all, avoid backhanders (the kind of compliment that ends up like an insult, such as, 'You did very well *for a woman* …' or 'You are looking wonderful *for someone of your age* …'). Remember that you are expressing your opinion, so phrase the compliment accordingly.

Consider the difference between 'That colour suits you' and 'I think that colour suits you'. Can you see that the first states a fact, and may, in the hands of an expert in colour coding, be proved right or wrong? The second is an opinion and is therefore always right. So 'You did that well' could change into 'I liked the way you did that' and so on.

 It is important to be **gracious** in giving compliments. Think of someone you have not paid a compliment to recently. It may be someone in your family. Write down in the space provided an idea for a compliment (any positive opinion you have of something that person is, or has done, or any word of appreciation) which you know would help the relationship. Then decide when you are going to deliver it. Make a point of paying this compliment within seven days. You may have to call on, phone or write to that person. But do make sure that you actually tell him or her in so many words what it is that you appreciate so much.

COMPLIMENT:

_____

_____

_____

_____

Watchpoint

Be sure to give enough positive feedback to people, especially to those closest to you – they are the easiest to take for granted. And when passing compliments, do remove the sting that can so often be in the tail, as in 'You did that well, **but** ...'. Perhaps we believe that we need to keep on encouraging those close to us to do better and better and are afraid that if we don't include a 'but' they may stop growing or trying. While it is certainly true that we can encourage others by what we say, this is much more effectively achieved by 'clean' compliments than by devaluing what has been achieved.

Now think of something special you need to say to someone important to you. This one should not be a casual compliment, but something meaningful, and perhaps something that should have been said a long time ago. It may be to someone in your family, or someone you have taken for granted for a long while. Perhaps you need to appreciate one of your parents, or your partner. Make this exercise rather more difficult than the last one, so that you are able to see the amazing effect of a genuine and sincere compliment on a relationship that has become tired.

WRITE DOWN WHAT YOU WILL SAY AND WHEN YOU INTEND TO DO IT:

_____

_____

_____

_____

Now make sure that you actually do it!

Accepting compliments

For many of us accepting compliments is far more difficult than giving them. If you find this difficult, think for a moment about why you feel uncomfortable.

WRITE DOWN SOME POSSIBLE REASONS:

_____

_____

_____

_____

Now examine these for rationality. Are you perhaps being unkind to those who compliment you? A compliment is a gift, and just as we would not throw a gift back into the giver's face, so too with compliments – we would be rude to throw them back at the giver as if they were of no value.

When you are at the receiving end of a compliment, try to bear these guidelines in mind:

- Acknowledge the compliment (and the person) with grace.
- Don't argue or disagree – an opinion does not have to be demonstrably true to be valid!
- Don't immediately return the compliment or change the subject.

Giggling, or being coy and embarrassed also doesn't help to make the event a happy one. Try this exercise to understand fully what I mean:

 Think about the way you accept compliments, then ask a friend to help you with this role play. One of you pay the other a compliment; for instance, 'I love that tie/dress you are wearing', and note how it feels if the other then responds with, 'What, this old thing? I've never been crazy about it myself ...'. The person giving the compliment will feel put down and hurt. That kind of response suggests that the one who paid the compliment has no taste, or is ignorant. Hardly a kind, appreciative response!

Reverse roles and try another kind of response that doesn't work well, such as, 'So what are you after?' as if the other person would only pay a compliment in order to get something, or 'That's what they all say', which is a silly reply that brushes off the compliment and makes a joke of it. All these insult the person who has, after all, been kind to you.

Often it is only when you do an exercise like this that you understand quite how these responses come across, and there may be one or two of your own usual responses among the ones you tried out. Make a **conscious effort** to be gracious and to accept compliments when they are given you, by saying, 'Thank you'.

It often happens that the person you are complimenting does not receive it graciously. You may find yourself put down, or suspected of having ulterior motives. Note how it feels to have your compliments dealt with in this way. It doesn't feel good, does it? So when you are complimented, try to remember how **you** felt about a negative response. And remember that each compliment you receive is a gift – accept it as such.

When in doubt

When you suspect (or it seems quite plain) that someone is being sarcastic and trying to be hurtful, *apply the same rules as if you knew he or she were serious* and still accept the compliment gracefully and at face value. It will completely take the wind out of the other person's sails if he or she is in fact trying to be hurtful. On the other hand, if you were mistaken and it was in fact kindly meant, you will not have hurt the other person. Either way you come out with dignity and grace.

Record it

Lastly, buy yourself a 'Compliments Book' – any hardcover exercise book that you can keep, with a pen, next to your bed. At the end of every day, try to remember any compliments you have received, and write them in your book, with the date. When the time comes (and it will!) that you feel low, or unappreciated, or a failure, **read your book**. It will do wonders for your self-esteem and for your view of life!

CHAPTER 8

Accepting the Rough without the Smooth

*It is salutary to train oneself
to be no more affected by censure than by praise.*
W SOMERSET MAUGHAM

How do you react when someone says to you: 'Now I really don't want to speak out of turn, but …' or 'I would be absolutely the last person to hurt or upset you, but …' and this is followed by something quite devastating? Very often it is something that they 'feel you ought to know'.

CONCENTRATING ON NEGATIVES

Isn't it funny how people who often don't even know you all that well may feel obliged to decide for you what you do or do not need to know? Particularly the negatives? And isn't it equally strange that while we have such difficulty believing the compliments we receive, or taking seriously the good things people say about us, we immediately believe as gospel truth all the bad things people say?

Someone says to you, 'You're such a talented person. You're warm, loving, understanding, artistic, musical, a wonderful friend, and although you are not always the most organised person, you are one of the most special people I know.' You glow for a moment or two, then begin to worry. 'So she thinks I'm a disorganised person. My life is a mess, and people have noticed. Maybe others talk about it when they mention me, and they say, with scorn or (worse still) pity in their voices, '"What a shame!"' You begin to apologise for things, and see what you do and don't do in a different light.

Your previous achievements and successes in organising things are suddenly tarnished and you wonder if your standards are so low that you only thought things were going well, while in fact people had merely been kind to you, humouring an incompetent.

Or you wear your wonderful new outfit, feeling gorgeous, and someone says, 'You've put on a bit of weight, haven't you?' Suddenly the outfit is all wrong, you feel lumpy and stupid for having chosen it and your day is ruined.

Somehow the negative things others say are far more credible than the positive things. And that should not be so.

OPINIONS ARE A MATTER OF FREEDOM

We've discussed opinions and the right all people have to hold their own opinion on everything, whether it is right or wrong. But we are free to choose whether or not we agree with any opinion expressed by any person.

What we think of something depends on a great many factors, many of them the result of our experiences and our upbringing. I cannot possibly like all the things you like, nor need we agree on any matter of taste. So if there is something that I like and you do not, that simply says something about our differences in taste and nothing at all about the matter as such.

Similarly, if you dislike something I have or do, it says something about who we both are and what we consider nice or nasty, and nothing at all about what I have or do. I can make up my own mind about what I think about your dislike in terms of my own standards, and these will differ, in some respects at least, from yours.

DIFFERENT PEOPLE, DIFFERENT STANDARDS

One of the things parents find so very difficult to accept is that their children will develop standards that do not, in all details, match their own. This is because their children's 'logic bubbles' (see page 24) will be different, and their interpretations of events will be different. Their experiences of school and social events outside the home, as well as the influence of friends and other people, will be quite outside the control of the parents and will also have an effect on the children's values.

That is not to say that the standards of the children will necessarily be inferior in any way to those of the parents. Frequently they are, in some respects at least, higher. But parents may feel threatened by what appears to be a loss of control and an upsetting of all they hold important.

> If there is anything that we wish to change in the child,
> we should first examine it and see whether it is not
> something that could better be changed in ourselves.
> C G JUNG

NEGATIVE OPINIONS

Sometimes at work or at home it is important to reach consensus so that a plan of action can be agreed on. Then there has to be negotiation, and someone may well have to give way. But that does not mean that anyone has 'lost', or that anyone's opinion is wrong. It is simply a matter of expediency and next time it may well run the other way.

Too often teamwork is made difficult by the fact that people become defensive of their opinions, identifying themselves with what they believe. They feel rejected or insulted if others disagree with them, and especially if they are outvoted. If you find yourself doing this, you will need to apply the tests of rationality to your underlying beliefs (see page 69), and discover why it is that you feel that *you are your opinion*.

Essentially, we need to hold on to two truths in this respect:

■ I am free to agree or disagree with others, whether their opinions are positive or negative, and whether they refer to me or anything else.

■ I cannot judge others by my own standards. If I must make a judgement at all, I should allow that judgement to be in relation to **their** standards – why, after all, should they behave in accordance with what I think is right? Who says I am?

Some people find undeserved criticism worst; I find it harder when there is good reason for the criticism. Then I feel awful – so exposed and discovered!

Even when we know that criticism is merely an opinion, it is nevertheless difficult to cope with it when it comes our way. Think for a moment about what you find most difficult to handle. Identify one or more negative things that have been said to you that you remember and that have hurt you. They may belong to a time long ago or they may be more recent.

WRITE THESE DOWN:

_____

_____

_____

_____

_____

Can you see any sort of pattern? Can you discover what kind of criticism is most awkward for you?

DEALING WITH NEGATIVE OPINIONS

Just as compliments are simply positive opinions others have of us, so criticism expresses the negative opinion others have of us or of something we have done. The same rules apply for both situations. People have the right to their opinions, and you are not obliged to accept or reject any opinion. The difficulty lies in the fact that most of us have a knee-jerk reaction to criticism, and our reaction can effectively block any further communication.

Being defensive

This knee-jerk reaction is usually to defend ourselves – to argue or make excuses. We tend to rush in with explanations and try to plead extenuating circumstances.

Constructive communication takes place when you are able to respond rationally and realistically, when you do not need to become defensive, do not suffer guilt and anxiety, and are not at the mercy of those who criticise in order to manipulate you.

If you want to achieve this state of affairs, you will need to put in quite a bit of practice. At first it may be very difficult to get past that instinctive urge to defend – to make excuses. Each time you manage to hold back, however, you will find it that much easier the next time. So make a conscious effort, even when you have exceptionally good reasons for what you have done, to keep quiet about them unless someone asks.

Why people criticise

Let's go back to look at our model again (see page 28) and see how criticism appears in each of the groups.

The reasons people have for giving negative feedback (criticism) are many. If their behaviour falls in Group 1, criticism may serve to point out perceived error, or to make them feel superior, and it may occur without any thought for the feelings of others. Someone whose behaviour falls in this group may often lash out with criticism such as, 'Stop it! You're spoiling everything!' or 'That's wrong! Do it like this', or 'You're no use to man or beast. Let me do it!'

In Group 2, it might be intended to embarrass, to break down, to induce guilt or anxiety, to manipulate, or simply as a form of revenge. You may hear sarcastic comments such as, 'Well look who's not so perfect after all', or 'You did a fine job, I must say', or 'Is that your best shot?!'

As we have seen, criticism very seldom occurs in Group 3, and if it does, it is more an apology than a criticism. People whose behaviour falls in this group might say something like, 'You're so much better at this than I am, but I wonder if it shouldn't have a teeny bit more salt?'

But in Group 4, the criticism will be for the benefit of the other person, to achieve an improvement, for growth, and to improve the relationship. Here criticism is likely to refer to something which at that moment prevents things from being as good as they might be, for example, 'I find it irritating if you leave your wet towel on the bathroom floor. Please will you hang it up each time?' This opens the way to a happier coexistence all round.

How people criticise

The way criticism is formulated in each group is also interesting. The Group 1 form will be aggressive – naming, blaming and shaming. It may be sharp or quite gentle, but it is likely to be fairly direct and not considerate of others' feelings. Examples of this could be, 'Idiot! Now look what you've done!' or 'You're driving me mad with your constant banging. You're a menace!' or 'Get lost, pest!'

Criticism in Group 2 will be veiled, indirect, often merely hinted at, or else on behalf of others: 'Of course, I wouldn't have said so, but other people have commented …' or 'You know what people are saying about you …?'

In Group 3, criticism is likely to be couched in compliments, or it may sound a bit like a confession: 'I know I shouldn't mind, but …' or 'It's nothing really, just my own bad temper, but …' or something along these lines. There will also be plenty of rescuing: 'I know it's not your fault' or 'You try so hard …'.

In Group 4, the criticism will be brief, clear, direct, relating to a behaviour or action (something that can be changed) and will be expressed as an opinion, often starting with 'I', as in 'I don't like it when you …'.

Manipulative criticism

The question of manipulation is one that needs looking at very thoroughly, since a great deal of criticism falls into the category of trying to get others to do things a particular way, either by shaming them, frightening them or appealing to some arbitrary set of 'rules' known only to the speaker. Our parents used this when we were young, and too many people use this kind of criticism in their marriages and close relationships, as well as at work. Manipulative criticism, or the absence of it, is what creates a negative or positive culture in the workplace or at home. Manipulative criticism also forms the basis of many (exploitative) work contracts and relationships.

Consider these, for example:

- 'Nobody wears that colour these days.'
- 'It's not right to say that.'
- 'You shouldn't do that.'
- 'Everyone knows that's wrong.'
- 'You've got to do it like this.'
- 'What got into you? How could you do that?' What made you think that you would get away with it?'

In all these examples there is an assumption that there is an external value system to which the speaker is appealing, and which applies equally to everyone. If you didn't know that, then you are obviously stupid, uninformed or badly brought up. Few people wish to appear stupid or ignorant, so they tend not to argue, and the manipulation succeeds.

Manipulative criticism can be dealt with by using the 'fogging' technique which is described below, since this defuses what may otherwise be hurtful, and frees the person who is being criticised to respond in a way he or she wishes. Criticism is often hurtful, so we don't want to allow it to get under our skin. Fogging is an excellent way of deflecting it without having to give it any serious consideration at all.

Fogging

Fogging is a technique developed by Manuel Smith and described in his useful book *When I say no I feel guilty*. This technique distances the 'victim' from what is being said, and devalues the comments being made. It tends to stop the other person very quickly, but could also lead to a high level of anger in them, so it should not be thoughtlessly used. It should not be used between, say, a husband and wife, but could be used in a more distant relationship, or in one where you actually want to develop some distance.

There is no honest self-disclosure in it and a relationship will not be enriched by the exchange, nor will the person making the manipulative remarks be encouraged to become more assertive instead of manipulative. But it is probably the most effective way of **desensitising yourself** to hurtful or manipulative criticism.

The fogging technique does not set up a win-win situation.

To fog, agree with anything the other person says that is true, agree with any possible truths and agree in principle. Do not answer any questions with factual replies. Concentrate on the words the person is saying rather than the meaning, to find something that you can agree with. It may be a seemingly unimportant word or phrase.

For instance, if the other person says, 'You're a good-for-nothing layabout. You never do anything worthwhile. You just sit around waiting for people to do things for you!', it may all be quite unjustified. But you might be able to say, 'You're right. I do spend a lot of my time waiting'.

You will have found something that is true to agree with, and the rest of the comments disappear.

Or you may prefer to say, 'Yes, layabouts don't do anything worthwhile. You're quite right. They do sit around a lot.' Again, you will have found something, this time something that is true in general, to agree with and will have ignored the rest, along with the personal implication. You will be amazed at how this technique protects you from being hurt. It operates like a shield that stops any hurtful message from getting through to you. You will even be able to cope with nasty comments about your parents or your moral standards – all the remarks that usually get you steamed up!

Avoid sarcasm though, since this is defensive, and when you become defensive it immediately opens you to hurt. Concentrate on the words rather than the meanings, as this will eventually desensitise you to criticism. For a very full treatment of this technique accompanied by wonderful examples, do read Manuel Smith's book. In fact, fogging can be fun!

Constructive criticism

Genuine **constructive criticism**, on the other hand, needs to be evaluated, perhaps discussed, and certainly explored. There is value in it, and we need to gain all we can from negative feedback that is given for our benefit.

How can you tell the difference? The difference between the two is for you to decide depending on the situation. Generally speaking, the rule of thumb is that genuine criticism will stand up to further enquiry and yield further, useful insights, while manipulative criticism will either fizzle out or change ground all the time.

Further enquiry

Further enquiry leads to specific criticisms, helps you to understand and change problematic behaviour, and at the same time helps others learn how to deal constructively with you. Questions you may ask in further enquiry are the following:

- 'What did I do that upset you?'
- 'What is it about … that irritates you?'
- 'Is there anything else that I am doing that makes you mad?'
- 'What could I do to improve/set … right?'

All of these questions encourage the criticiser to focus on the **behaviour** rather than on the **moral judgement,** and help in bringing perspective to the exchange. Can you see that constructive criticism will stand up to this, while manipulative criticism won't?

DELIVERING CRITICISM

When criticism is assertively given, it is brief, specific and relates to behaviours and matters that can be changed. There is absolutely no point whatsoever in criticising people about something they cannot change. If I say, 'I hate tall people' to someone who is two metres tall, I am not doing anything worthwhile. That person has no control over his height.

Similarly, people's background, language, colour, sex and personality are not matters which warrant criticism. We should also take ownership of (accept responsibility for) our criticism. It should start with 'I …' as an opinion and should relate to only one issue at a time.

Straight talk versus camouflage

It is interesting to note that the old idea of always initiating criticism with a compliment or affirmation may well be more damaging than helpful. Consider what it is that people usually remember if, in a string of compliments, one less than flattering remark is made! In fact, beginning with an affirmation may serve to add such weight to the criticism that the person you address may suspect that the matter is far worse than it seems, otherwise it would surely not have been necessary to dress it up so much!

There were two supervisors in a particular office, both of them women. One was very direct and would simply say to her staff, 'I don't like the way you did that report. I would prefer it to be tabulated. Please fix it up and bring it back to me as soon as you can.'

The other would call the person into her office and commence with, 'You have been delivering some very good work lately and I am very pleased with you. Also, I have noticed how pleasant you are to other staff in the office. Thank you.' Then she would go on to the matter in hand. 'However, this report is not quite the way I want it. I would rather it was tabulated. Do you think you could manage to do it again and bring it to me as soon as possible?'

> *The second sounds so friendly and sweet, but the truth of the matter is that the staff members far preferred the first approach. When asked what they didn't like about the second supervisor, some said, 'She is insincere. Why say all those good things when she is criticising your work? We never know what she really thinks.' Others said, 'All the time she is saying the nice things, I am waiting for the "but".' Still others said, 'She makes such a big deal out of things. If it is not such a big deal, why does she have to go to such lengths to soften it?'*

This is equally true in all relationships – both at home and at work.

It is preferable to deal with positive and negative matters separately and give each its full value. If you feel it is necessary to tell people you are criticising that you appreciate them as well, rather get the criticism out of the way first, and then, maybe, at a later occasion, commend them.

The double bind

In the same way, being apologetic may cloud the issue, and may even be manipulative. It might place people you criticise in a 'double bind'. A double bind means that whatever they do, it will be wrong, or they will feel guilty. Consider this example:

> *'I love you very much. In fact I love you more than my own life, and I would never do anything to hurt you. Please forgive me for this: I really don't want to hurt you, but I need to tell you that you …'*

The person who is receiving the criticism is required to be grateful for the great love even if what is said is horrible. This means that they are not permitted to be angry about what they are being told, or about the hurt they feel. To reject the criticism would be to reject the love so freely offered! To feel the hurt would be to call into question the integrity of the speaker! People have no defence against damage offered in this way.

Don't rescue

Be wary of the fallacy of 'rescuing' people. That happens when the criticism is softened by offering excuses in advance. Consider this, for instance: 'I know you meant well, and you have been under a lot of pressure lately, but you handled that situation rather badly.'

The implication of rescuing is that the person will not be able to cope with the criticism and you have to rescue them from the possible hurt. This is obviously an insult, and does not allow people being criticised the freedom to respond in their own way and at their own level. Treat people as adults and allow them to respond for themselves.

Think about how you could best put into words something negative you need to say to someone. Remember that, from your point of view, it is always better to have things out in the open; from the point of view of the relationship, things will become more real and rewarding if nothing is hidden; but also remember that there is a price on everything and the price of saying what you need to say may be higher than you really want to pay. Only you can decide.

WRITE DOWN YOUR CRITICISM:

_____

_____

_____

_____

There may well be something you need to do during the next few days in terms of speaking the truth to someone. If there is, then don't put it off.

Think about what it is and how to say it. Check that you are using Group 4 methods – that it is brief, to the point, dealing with only one issue, and it is not complicated by any rescuing. Then do it. You may want to practise it a bit with someone you trust if you expect it to be very difficult.

Write down what you would say:

_____

_____

_____

_____

HANDLING CRITICISM

Why is it that we tend to react to criticism with such anxiety and distress? It could be that criticism calls up earlier messages we have stored in our Parent state, which tell us that we are not (yet) competent, or acceptable in society, or perhaps even not loveable.

Certainly most of us react to more than the actual criticism of the moment. There are times when we feel that it is all too much, when we say, 'I can't do anything right' and 'Everything I try is a failure'.

Probably what underlies much of our distress is the fear that if people 'find out' about us, they will either no longer accept us, or will never trust us again. If other people discover the truth about us, that we fail and make mistakes, and often get things wrong, they will have reason not to believe in us. So we are constantly protecting ourselves from exposure, trying to convince others that we did not make a mistake, perhaps even that we meant to do things their way! Our failures must not be broadcast in case people get the 'wrong idea' about us!

Instant defence

This leads us into the trap of immediate defence, of excuses and attacking the criticiser:
- 'You can talk …!'
- 'But it wasn't my fault …'
- 'If only you knew …'
- 'It's not fair …'

Criticism from someone who is close to us, or important to us, whose opinion we value, also feels very much like **rejection**, and we often confuse 'I do' with 'I am'. If they criticise something we have done, we receive it as a criticism of what we are, and that is perceived as a rejection of ourselves.

Our normal response to that is to try to stop it as fast as possible or, at the very least, to explain why they should not think so badly of us.

Criticism is, as we said earlier, an opinion, and we may agree with it or not, as we see fit. The fact that someone else says it does not make it true. In fact, we may know considerably more about the matter than they do, especially when it is about ourselves!

Honest admission

When people criticise you honestly, you may want to deal with their criticism as follows:

- Listen to what they are really saying.
- Make sure you understand exactly what they are referring to (further enquiry, see page 118).
- Evaluate your response to the truth or otherwise of what they say.

If you agree with what has been said, acknowledge the criticism as valid and work towards a resolution: is there some way in which it can be put right?

If you do not agree, say, 'No, I don't agree …' then affirm the truth as you see it, clearing the way for constructive communication.

When Robbie, son of the company's owner, was brought into the office and placed in a responsible position, many people's feathers were ruffled. Robbie compounded this feeling by behaving irresponsibly and relying on the fact that his dad was the boss to get away with his poor showing. One particular Friday in summer, the call of the beach was too strong and he went off, completely ignoring the fact that there was an important meeting he needed to attend.

In our Communications Course group that Saturday, he mentioned the fact that he would probably be summoned to his manager's office first thing on Monday morning. We asked him how he would handle it.

'I'll make up some excuse,' he said, flashing his charming smile. 'Like what?' asked one of the group.

'Oh I don't know. I'm pretty good at making up stuff.' 'Will it work?' I asked.

'I don't suppose they can really do anything,' he smiled again. 'Let's role-play it,' I suggested.

I played the manager and Robbie played himself. Each time he came up with something, I shot him down and trapped him in his lies. Eventually, he said:

'It doesn't look as if it will work too wel, does it? What should I do?'

We suggested that he simply tell the truth. He was shocked, but agreed to try and we role-played his new reaction.

Playing the manager, I said, 'You were not here on Friday afternoon and you missed the meeting. That is highly irresponsible behaviour and I am very disappointed in you.'

Robbie now used the steps we suggested for dealing with criticism, evaluated whether the criticism was valid, found that it was, and replied, 'Yes, you're right. I am sorry. I wasn't here and my behaviour was foolish and unworthy of my position. I will not do it again.'

*When Robbie put this into practice, the manager was stunned. He had expected the usual ducking and diving from Robbie. He was so impressed with this new honesty and the way Robbie **accepted responsibility** for what he had done that he took no further action.*

What had been a very difficult relationship between the two of them began to improve from that time on.

If criticism is valid, admit it and make some suggestion as to how you intend putting right what was criticised. But if the criticism is not valid, then say so. It is never necessary to put yourself down, nor to accept criticism that is not valid, nor to allow yourself to be shaped in a way that you don't feel comfortable with.

Generally, avoid defence, which always involves explaining **why**: it tends to raise your own anxiety levels and it also brings in a whole bunch of other matters which may have no immediate bearing on what is being criticised. If you can cope with the criticism, face it. If not, use the fogging technique.

Never use people's criticism of you as an excuse to start criticising them. Do one thing at a time, and use genuine criticism as a **tool for growth.** It takes courage to criticise honestly those you love. So appreciate it when someone you love takes the trouble. A lot more would be achieved in relationships, and many people would grow a great deal more, if we took the trouble to be as honest about the negatives we see as we are about the positives!

How does this apply to you? Think about the insights you have gained in this chapter, that may be of use to you later on. What advice would you most want to remember from this chapter?

Are there particular situations that occur regularly which you are at present not handling well? What could you do to improve them?

WRITE THESE DOWN:

_____

_____

_____

_____

_____

_____

_____

▼

CHAPTER 9

Anger, Frustration and Resentment

*If you are patient
in one moment of anger
you will escape a hundred days of sorrow.*
CHINESE PROVERB

What may begin as a fairly harmless irritation or frustration, if it is not expressed and dealt with, may turn into a deep anger and, if still kept bottled up, may become a long-standing resentment and a barrier to effective communication.

HOW WE DEAL WITH ANGER

Anger is one of our most powerful emotions. It can be a positive, energising emotion, or it can destroy people. When it is not properly directed and used constructively, it can do much harm. It might even lead to illness – it reduces the efficiency of our immune system.

Unresolved anger and has been known to contribute to many health problems – colds and flu, aches and pains, even cancers and other serious illnesses. Pent-up anger almost always leads to alienation and unhappy relationships.

> I was irritated, but I preferred not to say
> anything; I became angry, and I managed not
> to say anything; then my resentment took
> over and I found I was unable to say
> anything. My body spoke for me
> in symptoms and pain.

Anger cannot be ignored

When an emotion such as anger is not allowed an outlet directed at its source, it has to direct itself inward, and the one it punishes then is the self. Anger is a dangerous emotion to ignore.

When people tell you not to be angry, or to **control** yourself, they seem to give you the choice of bottling it up and destroying yourself, or behaving in an unacceptable way and expressing your anger. But it is not wrong to be angry. What could be a problem is **inappropriate** anger, **excessive** displays of temper, **physical violence** and **constant** rehashing of your dislikes and frustrations.

Anger, frustration and resentment are all emotions which **victims** experience. Look at the diagram in Chapter 2 again (see page 28). Can you see that anger could be felt by people who are behaving in the lower two groups – below the line – in the area of the victim? If you decide to do something and you do it, you do not feel angry. If it comes out wrong, you may well feel disappointed, but if **someone else**, or some other event **outside your control** messes it up, you may well feel angry, frustrated or resentful. Anger is associated with feeling powerless. You may also feel angry when you are at the mercy of your own carelessness and stupidity.

If you are not careful enough and dent your new car while parking it, you will be angry: you will wish with all your heart that the outcome had been different, but will be quite unable to do anything to undo what has happened. You will be a victim of your own carelessness. But you are likely to be even angrier if someone else does the same thing!

A desire to have things different, along with a sense of helplessness, injury, often injustice, and varying degrees of resignation or a desire for retribution are what make up these emotions. You are angry when things are not what you think they should be and there is someone (or something) to blame.

THINK OF SOME OF THE THINGS THAT MAKE YOU ANGRY. WRITE THEM DOWN AND SEE IF YOU CAN ISOLATE THE PRINCIPLES OR THE PATTERNS THAT APPLY TO THEM:

_____
_____
_____
_____
_____
_____
_____

Do you find it easy to group the sources of your anger into categories? Is there something common to many of them? It may be that there is something that acts as a trigger to your worst feelings of anger. Sometimes this relates to an incident or incidents in your childhood, so that when someone does something similar, you experience all the pent-up rage of that past event along with what properly belongs in this moment. It would be worthwhile to discover what that incident was and deal with it, so that you don't need to feel the full load of rage every time.

Blame

When we do not feel free to accept responsibility for our own failures and mistakes, we will find something or someone else to blame, and anger and resentment will result. Many of us find it hard to accept responsibility for our own mistakes, perhaps because we have not given ourselves permission to get things wrong.

We even perpetuate this with our children. You may have heard parents or well-meaning adults teaching a child to shift the blame in **any** direction other than where it belongs. A small child may be taught to 'Smack the naughty chair that bumped you' when the child has in fact bumped into the chair.

Early conditioning like this certainly contributes to the 'victim mentality' so many people have, and to their inability to accept themselves and others as they are, complete with weaknesses. They will, as long as they are victims, battle with inordinate or inappropriate anger, resentment and frustration.

Helplessness

Perhaps the biggest component in inappropriate or inordinate anger is the sense of complete helplessness. If it is entirely the chair's fault that your leg is bruised, what on earth can you do about it? But if, on the other hand, you are responsible for bumping into the chair yourself, there is something you can do to avoid doing it again. Immediately the helplessness is gone, the feeling of being a victim is gone with it, and the level of anger is reduced. There is nothing that upsets us as much as being helpless in the face of what we don't want.

> It is important to understand that taking responsibility for your mistakes is not the same as blaming yourself.

To accept responsibility is to admit that it was your doing. To lay blame is to bring the idea of *fault* into the situation – to say that it was your *wrong*doing. A value judgement such as blame makes you feel guilty, and there is really no cause to feel guilty about making mistakes, or getting things wrong.

Guilt

Our misunderstanding of guilt is the cause of so much confusion creeping in. Guilt is something we should all feel when we do something that is morally wrong: something unkind, dishonest, damaging, greedy. Feeling guilty is meant to cause us to stop and consider, and then to change direction. It is our early warning system that we are about to do something wrong. Guilt is **not meant to be carried**, and applied to mistakes and mishaps. It is a destructive emotion and must be dealt with as a matter of urgency. We may safely accept that we will often fail. Being perfect is not a normal human characteristic and we are allowed to be imperfect.

It may be comforting to know that it is not your perfections that make you loveable, but your imperfections. Think for a moment of the person or people you love best. What is it that you particularly love about them? Their great successes? Their perfections? Or their funny little ways? Success and outstanding goodness or achievement make us worthy of respect and admiration, but our little failures make us lovable.

> I cling to my imperfection
> as the very essence of my being.
> ANATOLE FRANCE

Not that we set out to fail! But we should say to ourselves when we foul up, which we are bound to do several times in our lives, 'Welcome to the human race! Now you are normal!'

Making mistakes should not make you feel guilty. But do take note when there is reason to feel genuinely guilty and let that warning system play its part. Nasty, dishonest, greedy, unkind and self-centred acts do not make you loveable at all, nor are they useful at home or at work.

Finding the source

So before you start blaming other people or circumstances for your failures, get your facts right and discover whether your anger is in fact your responsibility or not. If it is, rejoice in your mistake, your humanity, your normality, and put right what you can. It is enormously important for us to get things wrong from time to time.

The best and most solid learning and development will come from our own mistakes, if we are prepared to face them and allow them to be a positive factor in our lives.

Finding a resolution

The first course of action is to put right what you can and forgive yourself for the rest. That does not mean pretending that nothing is wrong: it means acknowledging to yourself what you did, naming it properly and accepting the consequences of that action. But do not punish yourself for it. Consequences are usually sufficient punishment in life.

If an incident is not something for which you are responsible, then the second course of action is to discover whose responsibility it is. It will be as well to direct your anger to the right place. Again, be sure of your facts so that appropriate anger is expressed. You may need to take some time to cool off and gain a realistic perspective before you make the appointment to see, or before you write to, the person concerned.

Always try to give them warning if you can. Remember that you are looking for a **resolution**, not for **retribution**. At worst you will merely be able to express what you feel, and hope to prevent another occurrence. At best, you will be able to work through the entire incident and find a solution to the damage done, and at the same time keep, or even gain, a friend. Both ways you will not suffer the extra pain of continuing anger, frustration, avoidance and tension.

 Facing the person you believe is responsible for your anger may be difficult. Let's look for a moment at what the beliefs (self-talk) are that often make you want to avoid confrontation.

WRITE DOWN WHAT YOU THINK HOLDS YOU BACK FROM EXPRESSING YOUR ANGER APPROPRIATELY AND SIMPLY SAYING WHAT IS ON YOUR MIND:

_____

_____

_____

_____

_____

Consider the rationality of each factor. It may indeed be true that the people concerned will fight back, or use anger against you, or change their opinion of you. Weigh up the possible alternatives. What is their opinion of you now? Which will ultimately be more damaging – holding on to the anger and all that it causes, or taking the risk of some unpleasantness? Remember that if you don't at least express your anger, you may find yourself in Group 2. Do you really want to be pushed into passive manipulating behaviour in addition to the damage that has already been done? Probably not!

If you are unable to express your anger in some way, even if it is not to the person concerned, it will turn inward and begin to destroy you. There is no value in pretending that it has gone away when it is merely buried.

> *When we discussed old angers in a course one day, Maria said she could think of something she had been very angry about, but that it was no longer an issue. I asked her to tell us about it. While she was speaking, I noticed that her hands were fidgeting with her pen, and her face had become flushed.*
>
> *'How do you feel now?' I asked.*
>
> *'Quite all right. I simply decided not to think about it again,' she replied.*
>
> *'Did you notice that when you were speaking, you became agitated?' I asked.*
>
> *She put her hand to her chest. 'Yes, now you mention it,' she replied. 'My heart is beating faster and I feel hot.'*

Maria had thought that the feelings of anger had dissipated because she had refused to acknowledge them, but in fact they were waiting, stored away in her mind. When she spoke about the incident, the emotions returned, and when anyone did anything to her that was similar, they added to what she felt at the moment and made it much worse than it would otherwise have been.

It would have been far better for Maria if she had weighed up the risks associated with confronting the person who caused her anger in the first place, and had decided to speak out, rather than paying the price of keeping her anger bottled up. It was fortunate that not too much time had elapsed since the incident and so the damage to her was not yet severe.

 Perhaps you need to decide whether you are able to confront people who have hurt or annoyed you, or whether you will take the risk of leaving the buried anger to do its damage. Think carefully before making your decision.

Professional help

The third course of action is that you could consult a psychotherapist or other professional counsellor who is trained to help you deal with anger that you cannot handle directly. The therapist will help you identify old angers which you may not be able to call to mind without help. (Some things are buried so deep that they are difficult to find, but that does not reduce their power to affect our lives. In fact, deeply buried angers are very often the most dangerous.)

This is a very good route to go, and psychotherapy is generally covered by medical aid, so it will not cost you more than you can afford. If your medical aid scheme does not cover psychotherapy, you might be able to negotiate with the therapist for a reduction in fees, or you could go to one of the state organisations. Either way it is very important to get help if you are struggling with unresolved anger.

If you are a member of a church, your minister may, if he or she is qualified, be able to assist you here as well as with your guilty feelings.

 Think for a moment about some incident that made you very angry with someone. Consider whether you could bring yourself to approach this person and talk about your anger. How would you go about it?

How to express your anger

When you do need to express your anger towards someone, try to stick to these guidelines:

- Be specific – focus on the behaviour that is the problem.
- Avoid wild words – emotionally charged words can close off the lines of communication. For instance, if you tell people they 'ruined' something when in fact what they did was spoil it or hurt it, you introduce much more emotion than is called for. Take a moment to think of other words that have the same effect: 'ridiculous' or 'fatuous' is far more charged than 'inappropriate', and so on. Say nothing that is not true, or that will need apologising for afterwards. Avoid, of course, the aggressive behaviours of naming, blaming and shaming.
- Take ownership of your anger – begin with 'I …'.
- Be sure of your facts before you begin.
- Don't allow the other person to manipulate you into feeling guilty for being angry. Your feelings are your response to a particular set of circumstances and the resolution you are asking for will ease them.

■ Don't go on and on – the thousand words treatment achieves little more than resentment on the other person's part.

As far as possible, use our 'magic formula':

I (FEELING WORD) WHEN YOU (ACTION OR BEHAVIOUR)
AND I WOULD LIKE (RESOLUTION)

Imagine that you ordered a particular article and paid a deposit on it, to be delivered in time for a special event. It did not arrive and your event was spoilt.

You could say, 'I was furious when you did not deliver on time and I would like my money back in full, with a letter of apology.'

Or suppose your partner keeps forgetting to replace the lid on the toothpaste and you are really cross because you keep on reminding him, to no avail.

You could say, 'I hate it and I get really irritated when you leave the cap off the toothpaste. I would like you to start putting it back. Is there anything that I can do to help you remember?'

This formula is specific, simple, owned, firm and open to negotiation. In each of the above examples, you are telling the others how you feel, and it is therefore not an attack on them.

If they choose to be offended, still stick with what you are saying, but help them to put their feelings into words as well, so that between you, you are able to come up with some suggestion of what to do to resolve the issue.

Identifying unresolved angers

You will probably find that once you have started digging up past hurts, they will continue to come out. This may be very disturbing, but if you can manage to confront these issues and work hard at finding a resolution, you will find yourself becoming progressively more and more free and empowered. It is the most wonderful experience.

Think of an old anger that you have never dealt with and that needs to be resolved. It may be from yesterday, from last week, or even from when you were little. There are bound to be several incidents that come to mind, and many things that need to be resolved. Even if you think there is nothing that can be done about it, identify it.

WRITE THIS DOWN:

_____
_____
_____
_____
_____

It is not possible to deal with them all at once, unfortunately, but it is good to make a start. Try to begin with something not too difficult and gain confidence from that.

Contact the people concerned and tell them what is on your mind, using our 'magic formula'. If you cannot trace them, or if the person has died, or if it would be inappropriate or hurtful to speak to them, use one of the following techniques to externalise your anger.

- Use a surrogate person – a therapist or trusted friend – who will play the part of the person who has wronged you.
- Write a letter to the person. You don't have to post it. Burning it when

you have finished writing it may in fact be a good, symbolic way of closing the matter.

■ Phone the person or send a tape-recording.

Whatever you do, once you have identified an unresolved anger, work to resolve it. **On no account must you bury it again**.

CHECK YOUR THINKING

The feeling that things are wrong or that they shouldn't be the way they are might arise from the facts of a situation, or it might be the result of an unrealistic, demanding attitude. When your self-talk persists with 'It's not fair!' in any of its forms, there is a strong possibility that you have hit some irrational thought. Examine it. You may find that the whole sense of helpless injustice will evaporate when you discover what is really causing it. Then you can begin to take responsibility for yourself instead of demanding 'fairness' from others. You may even discover that you are less a victim than the sad owner of a victim mentality!

 Are you measuring others by your own personal standards and expectations? Do you have the feeling that, because you have done most things right and are kind to others, life should treat you more kindly? Check the rationality of your self-talk carefully before feeding your hurt or anger (see page 69).

Particularly in South Africa today, with our history of very strong stereotyping on grounds of race and gender, and with the legislation that had flowed from these, there are many of us who carry immense loads of very deep anger and resentment. It is a tragedy to add to these rational loads the extra anger that comes from the habits of being a victim. It is urgent, therefore, for our own health and for the future of our country, that we each take responsibility for our actions, their consequences and our emotions, and deal with our rational feelings of anger.

Working on your own responses

There are some things that will never be put right. There are many things in the past which not only cannot be undone but also cannot be told to the person concerned. You may feel that some of these are not worth mentioning to anyone else. All we have to work on is our own response to these, and our wellbeing is our own responsibility anyway. If this is the case, the three areas you could work on in yourself are:

- Remember that unresolved anger is the emotion of a victim. Take control of your life more and more, and make you own decisions. Every time you take responsibility for yourself and make a decision which you can act on, you move your behaviour up above the line and your anger reduces because you are dealing with it.
- Check the rationality of your interpretation of the event (your self-talk) that makes you so angry and see if it feels better when you no longer expect others to reach your own standards of behaviour, or demand 'fair' actions.
- Work on feeding the positive pictures in your mind. Fill your mind as far as possible with things that are lovely, good, kind, noble, constructive; look at beauty and hold beautiful images in your mind; collect friends who are optimistic, and see how the 'climate' of your mind alters and affects the perceptions you form. Your interpretation of life is strongly affected by your overall view of whether this world is a nice or nasty place. But do not deny or try to ignore your real anger. This is a dangerous and destructive thing to do.
- Encourage yourself and be kind to yourself. Try to learn to love yourself and accept that changing takes time.

Accepting responsibility

Once you have decided to accept responsibility and work on your own anger, follow these steps:

- Listen to your self-talk and identify exactly what it is that you are angry or resentful about.
- If you cannot express the anger to the person concerned, find another person you can trust, or a professional who is trained to handle these confidences, and put your feelings into words.
- Together work out what, if anything, needs to be done to repair the damage, or what irrational thoughts have led you into this emotional cul-de-sac. Evaluate where you are and what might help you.
- Formulate a programme for yourself, including positive affirmations of your own worth, practical things to do and deadlines for their completion. List the positive signs you will probably experience as the old anger or resentment disappears.

▪ Gratefully deal with new irritations as they arise, before they can harden into powerful feelings that may turn you into a victim again.

If you are surprised that I use the word 'gratefully', then think about it. What can be better than being able to deal with events when they arise, and have them sorted out before they can become a source of pain and resentment!

A RIGHT TO REVENGE?

Dealing constructively with your anger cannot ever mean getting even with others. That is aggression, and it leads, along with other aggressive behaviour, to alienation, broken relationships and self-hatred.

Our aim in developing a constructive communication style is not to win at the expense of someone else, but to resolve the difficulty. Anger signals a problem. It will persist, whether consciously or unconsciously, until the problem has been dealt with. Honesty, forthrightness, clarity and good listening will go a long way towards achieving resolution, not retribution, and the sooner they can be well used, the cleaner and easier the result will be.

Don't fear your anger; don't hide your anger. Do **deal with it** and let it go. Give yourself enough time to respond appropriately and take the relatively small risk of facing what will otherwise destroy much that you hold dear.

> **The pain of healing,**
> **while not easy to cope with,**
> **is more bearable than the pain of hurt.**
> W A WOOD & L A HATTON

CHAPTER 10

Power Ploys and Games

Onlookers have a clearer view of the game
than the players.
SIR RICHARD LIVINGSTONE

In the previous chapter we discussed anger, and how much harm is done if you do not find a way of venting your anger, or processing it. We looked at some methods of dealing with our anger. In this chapter we are going to deal with another aspect of behaviour which is related to anger, namely power ploys and games people play at work and at home.

GAMES PEOPLE PLAY

Think for a few moments of some of the people at work or at home at whom you have directed your anger. What was it that they did (or did not do) that was so upsetting to you? You will probably find that many of them will have been **manipulating** you in some way or another. Your response of anger was the response of the **victim**.

 In the light of what you now know, do you have any ideas of how you can stop being a victim, and what you could do to prevent a great deal of anger from being necessary in the first place?

WRITE THIS DOWN:

_____
_____
_____
_____
_____

Look carefully at what you have written. Have you mentioned the principles of communication in Group 4? I hope so. If you have written something like, 'Say what I really think in an appropriate way,' or 'Express my anger immediately to the person concerned,' or 'Use the "magic formula" to put my feelings into words,' then I think you are well on the way to dealing with much of your anger before it becomes a problem – before it creates a silence barrier.

If, on the other hand, you are still inclined to run away, to avoid confrontation, or to give in to keep the peace, then there is still a lot of work to be done. You are a prime candidate for further manipulation and for being drawn into other people's games.

 Where you were caught in a 'double bind' (see page 119), you were perhaps not free to formulate your anger and express it against the person concerned. This may have resulted in feelings of inadequacy or guilt on your part.

WHAT CAN YOU NOW DO WHEN A SIMILAR SITUATION ARISES?

_____

_____

_____

_____

If you are not sure, read the chapter on dealing with anger once more.

Dishonesty

The basis for the power games people play in the work environment (or at home) is dishonesty. This means producing a situation in which things are not what they appear to be.

You may be led into a sense of false security by people who flatter and 'appreciate' you while they wait to trap you into some mistake or indiscretion. They are then able to use that to move you down and themselves up in the organisation. Once again, you would become the victim of their manipulation.

Or you may find that you are being left out of the information chain. Somehow you are not informed of a meeting you needed to attend, or there are plans afoot of which you know nothing.

You may even be given an extra area of responsibility and feel very good about it, until you discover that it is bound to be a disaster because of something that was done or omitted when a previous person was responsible for it, and you have been chosen to be the scapegoat when things go wrong.

This sounds dreadful, and might incline you towards disliking or fearing your colleagues. It is worth understanding, however, that personal malice is very seldom involved, and that this kind of behaviour is part of an ethic which operates because of a particular structural set-up. One often encounters this kind of power game in large organisations with pyramid structures, such as the civil service and big corporations. It seems that the structure itself has a lot to do with the existence of games. It is not our task to pass moral judgement on those who play them – there may be much more involved than is apparent. What this section aims to do is to help you understand why it is that you are sometimes placed in situations you hadn't expected, and how to deal with people at work when they want to use you in their own play for success or power.

In small companies, these power games seem to be far less in evidence, and may be absent altogether.

Dealing with power games at work

Supposing you discover that people in your own department are playing power games, and you run into rumours and hints, the kind of situation where what is *not* said seems to be more important than what *is* said, and you are expected to know what is behind it all. You will need to decide whether or not you are prepared to play along. If not, then read on.

Sincere further enquiry is a good place to start, as usual. When someone says, 'You know what I mean ...', one reply could be, 'No, what do you mean?' It is amazing how a situation can sometimes change when you really take time to ask and listen to someone. But unfortunately this is not always the case and sincerity may be met with derision or worse. If this is the case, the distance created by fogging (see page 116) may well be your best option.

But understand that there is a cost on everything. *Refusing to play games may not work to your advantage in the short term in a work situation or home environment where there is heavy game playing.*

You may in fact find that even management fails to appreciate your honesty and loyalty in trying to make things work really well and in chasing the truth. You may inadvertently dislodge the game that someone powerful is also playing! You must make the decision yourself, and do whatever it is that you are comfortable with. It is your life and you are the only one finally answerable for what you do.

Power games in the family

Interestingly enough, power games happen in families too. There are those who keep their spouse short of money and therefore always dependent and begging; there are those who humiliate their partner or their children in public. Very often these behaviours are the expression of anxiety and feelings of inadequacy. They are always very damaging to relationships.

The kind of behaviours we observed in Group 2 of our model (see page 28) also occur in these games. One of the more effective ways of dealing with these family games is to hold on to your determination to treat the person playing these games as an adult, and therefore to take whatever is said as true. If you ask, 'What's wrong?' when your partner is sulking and get a 'Nothing!' response, you could reply, 'I'm so relieved! I really thought you were upset about something. I'm so glad you're not.' Then go on as if there's no problem at all.

This will probably not help much in the short term (your partner may sulk for another day, week, month …) and it may not even succeed in the long term, but it is your best bet. It will get the message across that you are not prepared to play games. Stick with it and try to *maintain your sense of humour and your sense of your own self-worth at all costs.*

Why people play games

Game playing is sometimes a refuge for people who are insecure in their own estimation of their ability to succeed and who have the belief that there is a limited amount of success around. They have the idea that if anyone else is allowed to succeed, that diminishes the amount of success available for themselves.

The truth is quite the opposite; success breeds success, and the more people succeed, the more there is for everyone else. This is why really successful managers spend so much of their time helping their team to develop and to succeed.

In a happy marriage both spouses benefit from each other's success instead of their relationship being hampered by petty jealousies.

Games siphon off huge amounts of emotional energy (and very often time as well) and cause disruption and suspicion in relationships. Teamwork is the first casualty and priceless synergy is lost. People on the same team are unwilling to cooperate with one another in case someone else gains the advantage. You can see how the company (or relationship or marriage) suffers – there is no space for the advantage of the clients or the shareholders, or even for the long-term stability of the firm to be brought into the equation, just so long as nobody else gets the main benefit from the situation!

Openness, honesty and responsibility have the opposite effect, making it easier for everyone to do their work and freeing up energy for happy teamwork and productivity.

HOW TO AVOID PLAYING ALONG

The only way to stop game playing is to get matters out into the open and to hang on to your free responsible behaviour. Responding to manipulation with a confident, non-aggressive attitude has the best chance of hooking adult behaviour out of the other. When you become aware that there are tensions beneath the surface, try to flush them out with direct questions and further enquiry. For instance, you might say, 'I feel as if I am missing some of the real meaning here. Is what I am hearing (reflect back on what you have understood) the whole message? Am I being naïve?' Or, 'I sometimes get the feeling that you don't believe that what I say is true, and it seems that you don't always quote me accurately. I find this a problem and would like to find a way to solve it. What do you suggest?'

Note that there is no attack and no judgement, because you keep this in the area of perception. You perceive a problem – and there is no Parent-Child attitude – you treat the other person as an adult and call for suggestions on solving a problem which you have. In other words, your behaviour falls in Group 4. On the other hand, you have not pretended that this is all your own fault or just a matter of your own feelings, as in Group 3 – you have identified an action of the other person's as the likely source of your problem.

With this sort of approach there is a chance of both of you being able to say what you feel and of working out a solution. You will probably also gain respect and admiration as a person who is able to deal with things directly and you will be seen as a person who can handle difficult matters without putting others down. At every point others have the right to argue your perception, to deny a problem and back off, if they wish to take that course. That means that you may not be able to sort out the problem, but it is your best chance.

If you suffer a non-verbal put-down (like a 'dirty look' or someone turning his back on you when you approach), you are quite free to ask for an explanation. You may want to bring out into the open what that person is upset about. More often than not it is a misunderstanding, and the other person is unable to speak to you directly.

Rumours

When rumours circulate, don't pass them on. They almost always grow in the telling and are unlikely to be altogether true. In fact, they may really be false and may do a great deal of harm to the person concerned and to those who pass them on! As far as possible, ignore them, even though there is such a temptation to be seen to be in the know; sometimes it feels really good to know something that the others don't yet know. If it does seem important, then examine both the content of the rumour and its source.

As far as possible, deaal personally with the person concerned and involve as few people as possible. Rumours are a powerful way of spreading uncertainty and untruths anonymously and there is quite often a malicious intent behind them. Never passing on rumours is important if you want to spend your time operating in Group 4.

Divided loyalty

Avoid joining any 'camps'. By this I mean, when you can sense that people are forming factions – lobbying opinion or support against a person or group – then try not be on anyone's side. There is always a certain amount of manipulation of facts when this occurs. And at least one side is going to lose anyway – if not both! Of course there is nothing wrong with lobbying in itself, but when it is directed at a person or another person's career, have nothing to do with it.

The same applies at home and in families. Mom or Dad may try to get their children to side with them. Family feuds could last for years with families divided into different camps because of some insignificant incident which might have taken place generations ago. Nobody benefits from this kind of behaviour – it has an impoverishing and destructive effect on relationships.

POWER PLOYS – A REVIEW

Once again, you are free to decide for yourself whether or not you wish to be part of any other person's power game. It may be in your interest; it may not be. Only you can decide which relative cost you are prepared to pay. Power games rely on the roles of aggressor and victim to succeed. The person seeking power tries to achieve this by **disempowering** others: socially, emotionally, organisationally, through a lack of meaningful delegation, or by misrepresentation. There is a need to build up a comparison which favours the power-seeker, and which strengthens the myth that keeps others down.

If you decide that you will not play, try to stick to these rules:

- Keep things in the open: remember that very little can be achieved by the player if everyone knows what is really happening.
- Establish the real facts: don't be afraid to appear naive and even ignorant – it may be a lot safer.
- Accept no innuendoes and hints: chase the truth. People often rely on your unwillingness to look silly by asking exactly what they mean, and when you do, the whole shabby game is revealed.
- Ask questions of the player or players themselves: you are more likely to get closer to the truth, and you will at the same time show yourself to be someone who isn't easily manipulated.
- At work, use your reporting line and keep everything in writing: *never* complain about anything in your department to anyone in another department, however sympathetic they may appear. It will not be interpreted as a cry for help, but as disloyal, and will mark you as untrustworthy in the eyes of the listener as well.
- **Look for a workable compromise**. If you can be sure of a win-win solution then you have succeeded.

Keep your door open

Try to remember what was said by a wise old man some years ago: 'When you are right and the other person is wrong, give him/her a ladder to climb down on.' This operates in the same way as the Japanese idea of 'saving face', and is a way of allowing others to admit to being wrong while still maintaining their self-esteem. Where you cause others who are already uncertain of their worth to lose face, it is possible that their need to play the power games will increase rather than disappear. If you push people into a corner and so put them in a position where they are **forced** to admit that they are wrong, they are likely to try to fight their way out. Any cornered animal or person's first instinct is to fight. You may find that in the end you are worse off than they are – many a person in the right has been hurt because of forcing others into a no-win situation, causing them to become vicious.

Your acceptance of your own fallibility and the many times when you have got things wrong will help you develop compassion for the faults of others, and this will in turn allow you to be free from the need to prove others wrong and make them squirm. Openness and honesty, in yourself and with others, are the best immediate game-busters. In the long term, helping others by allowing them to build their own self-esteem will mean that fewer and fewer people will need to play games at all.

CHAPTER 11

My
Personal Plan

Communication in every form
is so much part of man as man
in the very depth of his being,
that it must always remain possible ...
KARL JASPERS

While working through this book, you will have many opportunities to put various of these ideas and suggestions to the test.

Practising the techniques will help you to be ready and able to use them when the opportunity arises.

Take all we have covered and think for a while about how you can put it to good use. Will you decide to read through this book over and over on a regular basis? Many people find that they discover facts they did not even know were there when they read something again after a while. We are only able to take in what is significant for us at the time.

What are you going to change immediately? What will you work on after a while? When? To whom are you going to apologise? Who are you going to confront? What will you be doing differently?

Turn over the page and draw up your personal action plan. Be as specific as you possibly can, and give some to what you intend doing. If you feel this is too embarrassing, or if you are afraid that someone else may pick up the book and read what you have written, either write in pencil so that you can rub out the tasks you have set yourself as soon as you have completed them, or use a separate piece of paper.

But I would recommend writing in the book. Pieces of paper get lost very easily, and in no time at all you may have forgotten what is so very clear to you now. Furthermore, if you write in the book itself, each time you pick it up and read it again, you will be reminded to do some more work on the behaviours you still show that are not helpful, or that could be made more effective. Your decision to work on improved communication and relationships may be one of the most important decisions you have made in your life, if you will actually do what you plan to.

Relationships that have been troublesome for ages may finally be put right, and your whole life may take on new meaning as you break the silence barrier. Certainly your stress levels will be significantly reduced and you will be both healthier and more able to cope with the normal strains of today's society.

Your future is to a great extent in your own hands. Do the best you can, and feel good doing it! Your greatest asset will be your increasing inner strength and confidence as you succeed in breaking old patterns that don't work, and developing new ones that help you grow in freedom as you communicate towards better relationships.

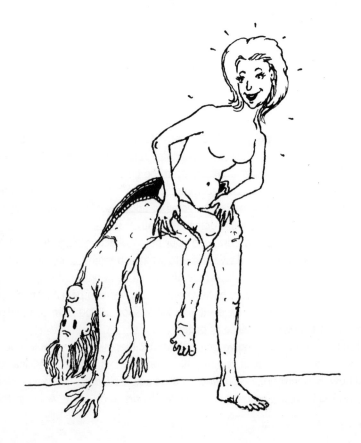

Action Plan

I used to want the words 'she tried' on my tombstone.
Now I want 'she did it'!
KATHERINE DUNHAM

_____
_____
_____
_____
_____
_____
_____
_____
_____
_____
_____
_____
_____
_____
_____
_____
_____
_____
_____
_____
_____
_____
_____
_____
_____
_____
_____
_____
_____
_____
_____
_____

Further Reading

Backus, William & Chapian, Marie, *Telling yourself the Truth*. 1985. Bethany House Publishers, Minneapolis.

Berne, Eric, *Games People Play*. 1986. Penguin Books, London.

Covey, Stephen R, *The 7 Habits of Highly Effective People*. 1992. Simon & Schuster, London.

Jeffers, Susan, *Feel the Fear and Do It Anyway*. 1991. Arrow Books, London.

Keyes, Ken, *A Conscious Person's Guide to Relationships*. Out of print but possibly available from libraries (New Dimentions Foundation, San Francisco).

Smith, Manuel J, *When I say no, I feel guilty*. 1975. Bantam Books, Toronto, New York.